Creativity is adult play

Childhood is an essential period of life to which everyone is entitled. It is the necessary foundation for adulthood. Children who grew up in alcoholic homes develop patterns of behavior and thought that minimize the pain and chaos, and optimize safety. Later in life, because they didn't have a chance to really be children, some ACOAs will find that they do not know how to play, how to be spontaneous.

Personally, I found my creativity and playfulness were blocked by frightful self-consciousness. I had taught myself how to act in a controlled way, and now I couldn't let go. The gradual return to playfulness and free creative expression has felt like an enormous step toward recovery and wholeness.

In a society that has become increasingly focused on production and accomplishment, we should all fear for the future of pure playfulness. As we speed ourselves up in the "search for excellence," we lose our sense of magic and abandon. I dread the loss of play not only because it signals the devaluation of fun for its own sake, but also because play, imagery, and creative endeavor provide people with important releases from stress.

From LITTLE MISS PERFECT

LITTLE
MISS
PERFECT

Megan LeBoutillier

BALLANTINE BOOKS • NEW YORK

ISBN 0-345-36283-7

This edition published by arrangement with CLAUDJA, Inc.

Manufactured in the United States of America

First Ballantine Books Edition: November 1990

DEDICATED TO:

*AUNT SARAH AND RUBYS SLIPPERS
WHO TAUGHT ME ABOUT GRIEVING.*

*AND FOR ALL ADULT CHILDREN OF
ALCOHOLICS
(ACOAs) AND THOSE WHO LOVE THEM.*

Contents

Acknowledgments

I have many people to thank for their generous help and support throughout the writing of this book. To Carol Philips, who encouraged me to "talk to the girls inside your head." To Larry Daloz, who initially helped with organization and concepts. To Kay Scott, E.B. & Paul Nelson, my sisters and many other friends for their untiring enthusiasm. And to all of my old and new friends who shared their stories, their fears and their hopes both informally and formally in the interviews. Thank you to Donna and Jim, Patrice, H.P., Denise, Susan, Kay, Alexandra, Judy and Eve.

Thank you to my parents for always doing the best that they knew how, and for leaving the window cracked open just enough for a breath of fresh air to get in.

Thank you to Jack and Claudia for their belief, support and suggestions.

And a very special thanks to Karen McMullen and Susan Barrett without whose help I might never have started or had the courage to take Mimi, Freeme, Little Miss Perfect and Megan on this journey.

Introduction

LITERATURE ON ALCOHOLISM IS FULL OF INFORMA-
tion supporting the notion that an alcoholic household is
more chaotic than others. The probability for confusion,
broken promises, and miserable holiday disappointments
is greatly increased in a family where alcohol is abused.
Young children are not equipped to understand why adults
behave in the ways they do. The changes in behavior, perhaps the violence, the forgotten birthdays are generally
beyond the reasoning powers of a child. As such, these
situations are stressful for the child. In reaction to feelings
of stress, children have a need to make everything seem
right, to make order from chaos. Various coping strategies must arise in response to the stress and confusion that
alcoholism presents to a small child.

Although I was certainly not consciously aware of the
stress that I was under as a child, I know that I did devise

a coping strategy for sorting out the chaos around me. I wrote children's stories, which were thinly veiled renderings of my own family. The plots helped me to explain what I could not understand within my family. I always provided happy endings to the stories, which also helped to ease my fears. Surprisingly, by the age of eight I already knew that I had better not show my stories to anyone. Somehow I knew that I was violating a family taboo, but I needed to do it. I chose to disguise the details and hide the evidence. I was trying to survive.

I would write the text of these stories in which everything turned out well in the end and where everyone was happy. My best friend, Amie, would draw pictures to accompany each page. We wrote and drew with colored pencils on specially cut-to-size paper and threaded bright ribbon through holes on the side as binding. It was a healing ritual for me as well as part of a dream. I knew, even then, that I wanted to be a writer someday. I wanted to be heard, without necessarily having to be seen.

One day I came home from school and discovered that my room had been violated. There were the carefully cut and colored pages of my stories, spread out on my bed like an accusation. They had been searched out and discovered within the empty cracker boxes—where I hid them on my bookshelves. I instinctively knew I would be called to explain their existence. I was afraid of the criticism, furious about the invasion of my privacy, and unable to fight back in any way. I wound up putting the stories and my feelings away for twenty years.

Later, as I returned to the process of writing as an

adult, I was surprised by the images of alcoholism that kept popping up. I began to draw a connection between my own self-consciousness with writing and the silencing that had taken place when I was a child. I came to suspect that alcoholism, more than writing or criticism, was the catalyst or important feature in my confusion.

On a walk one day with a friend, a writer, and also an ACOA, we spoke of our lifelong dreams of "being writers." We both followed this avowed desire with a litany of fears, self-doubt, and harsh criticism. Suddenly I made a connection. I thought of the children's story *The Emperor's New Clothes*. I looked at my friend and at myself and I saw bright, sensitive, and highly perceptive children who were taught to doubt their perceptions, deny reality, and keep their mouths shut. No wonder we were stifled by our self-imposed need to justify and explain. No wonder our words escaped us. I began to wonder about the creative process and the nature of growing up in an alcoholic family. I became obsessed with the notion of getting out from under the influence of family alcoholism. I wanted to know how other ACOAs felt affected both as children and as adults, and I wanted to know what they did with those feelings. Where had their childhood instincts led them, and where were their adult instincts leading them? Were they blocked, like me, by some incident from childhood? Were they blocked by something that they could not identify? Or were they blocked at all?

I began my research with a close, personal examination and a thorough study of alcoholism and the effects that it has on the alcoholic and the family system. In a book by Janet Woititz I was immediately affirmed in several of my suppositions:

ACOAs are afraid of being harshly judged.

ACOAs guess at what normal behavior is, and suspect that they never do anything right.

ACOAs overreact to changes over which they have no control.

While I felt exposed and vulnerable in accepting these realities about myself, I also began to identify the roots and causes of much of my confusion as a child and as an adult. Before this time, before dedicating myself to the process of recovery, I had blamed my parents or other adults for instilling the self-doubt that I suffered. I was a victim. I chose to blame and remain a victim rather than accept any responsibility for changing that which I did not like in myself and in my life. I began to define and identify the effects of a formative reality that was never mentioned, admitted, or explained to me as a child. I hoped that if I could understand it that I could then escape its hidden traps and expected responses. I wanted to be free of this unseen monster.

I decided to name all of the different aspects of myself that I could find, thus making those aspects truly a part of *me*. I owned them and was responsible for them. I tried to love them, even the parts that were not very lovable. Taking responsibility and accepting the process of working on myself was hard, but it freed me from the helpless position of victimization.

Introduction

I found that understanding alcoholism and its effects was just the beginning of the process of recovery.

I followed my personal self-examination with interviews with other adult children, in order to expand and confirm my observations. After a very short time people were calling me, asking to be interviewed. People whom I had never met. This was a surprise that convinced me of the strong need among ACOAs to break the imposed silence of their childhoods. The interviews illustrate the shared desperation felt by ACOAs and their struggles to be seen, heard, and to have fun as adults.

Little Miss Perfect represents my personal journey and struggle with issues associated with being an ACOA. My questioning and my creative need to express myself freely have led me, and are still leading me, on a journey of recovery. I hope that the material and the exercises in this book will help other ACOAs reacquaint themselves with their spontaneous, playful, and creative selves. It is my heartfelt wish that ACOAs in recovery can refashion their worlds to suit their own needs, and thereby get out from under the influence of family alcoholism.

I refuse to believe that I, or any other ACOA, am doomed to repeat or continue to react against alcoholic parental influence. I refuse to accept that children must continue to pay for the choices or diseases of their parents. I believe that through difficult self-examination, understanding, mourning and creative risk taking that any adult child can move from the automatic response childhood position of helpless victim into a healthier adult position of independence, self-love, and spontaneity.

I am thankful to those old and new friends I made throughout the process of working on this book and for their courageous efforts to help me dig deep—into their childhood minds. The friendships that have grown from this work have enhanced us all and helped us to release the frightened hold on our own victimization. I laugh as I see myself, and others whom I have worked with, regaining a healthy childlikeness.

PART ONE

As we grow up, looking around, trying to catch a look at ourselves in bits of mirror, children who grew up in alcoholic homes find that the mirrors around them are clouded. Often there are no alternative mirrors to look into, so the blurred images get accepted as "normal." It is time to provide clear lenses for those who want to see, rather than continue walking around in, and accepting a blur.

What
Went On
In There?

*D*URING A GUIDED IMAGERY SESSION WITH A THERA-pist eight years ago, I was instructed to enter a house and walk from room to room. My first reaction to the suggestion was, "What house? This is never going to work. I won't be able to see anything. This is weird." But, when I closed my eyes, there I was walking toward the front door of my childhood home. I went inside and wandered around. It looked as if no one lived there. All the furniture was covered with sheets. The therapist instructed me to find a mirror and to look at myself before leaving the house. The instant my image appeared I broke into deep sobs, and the mirror vanished, along with the house.

I was surprised to have entered that house and shocked to have such a strong reaction to my own reflection. Because I had gone to the therapist, I thought, for something quite unrelated to my childhood, I felt the experience was odd. I had gone in to explore my confusion about intimacy.

That day I made a conscious decision to leave the house and close the door tightly behind me. I was shaken and frightened. I didn't understand how I had wound up back there. However, I also promised myself that some day, when I was feeling stronger, I would go back through that house, tear off all the sheets and stand before the mirror in tears for as long as I needed.

In the intervening years I carried an image of Pandora's Box, believing that if I approached the house of my childhood, more painful surprises would come hurtling out. At the same time, as I struggled to understand myself I kept stubbing my toe on the corner of that same box. I knew pain from my childhood was there, unopened and in the way. This book is the chronicle of my journey and my efforts toward reclaiming my natural self through the process of recovery.

Until recently, alcoholism was one of the best kept secrets in this country. The collective hesitancy to accept alcoholism as a disease rather than as a failure of will has permitted a conspiracy to ignore alcoholism and its effects on the entire family system.

There are an estimated 28 to 34 million children of alcoholism and adult children of alcoholism living in the United States. That is a lot of people wandering around wondering, "What really went on back there?" The numbers also indicate that the potential for a great deal of support exists for anyone beginning the process of self-examination, mourning, and healing.

What Went On In There?

Within the typical alcoholic family there exists a strong spoken or unspoken code of denial and silence. The rules, stated or not, dictate that family members not talk, trust, or feel. The net effect of society's denial and the strict family code is a high degree of isolation, confusion, fear, and depression among family members. Individual children become invisible. Each family member's problems are ignored as the entire family is bombarded by constant, unexpressed stress and fear. Each family member is affected in a different way depending on age, position in the family, awareness of the problems, and the particular problem-solving style of the family.

Certain variables will determine how different family members respond to family alcoholism. The degree and observability of the drinking is one such variable. Did your alcoholic parent start drinking at breakfast, or follow the more accepted drinking practices of "social drinking"? Were there loud arguments in your house? Did the police routinely show up at your door, bringing your parent home when he or she was too drunk to drive? How did your other parent react?

The type of behavior exhibited by the alcoholic parent is another variable. When drinking, was your alcoholic parent belligerent, abusive, stupid, neglectful, or just plain absent? Each family member's perception of the situation will vary depending on his or her age at the onset of alcoholism. The effect on a child born into an alcoholic home will be more profound than for the adult whose parent slipped into the bottle after he or she left home for college, career, or marriage.

The entire family responds and adapts to the alcoholic in various ways over time. At first, family members will adjust their own behaviors in response to the behavior of the alcoholic. Children may stop inviting friends over or begin spending more time away from the house. Non-drinking spouses may begin creating excuses and justifications for the alcoholic's behavior. Individual family members strive for survival and the avoidance of conflict. The adaptations are typically not discussed, but rather they emerge in response to an unspoken situation. A family in this stage of reaction can continue to deny the existence of alcoholism. One disturbing characteristic is that family members perceive no other options. They are reacting to alcoholism and to the alcoholic without a clear vision of reality. The impulse is toward survival, and individual members back away, keep silent, deny the "problem," and numb their feelings. Many families never progress beyond this stage of reaction.

While these adaptive behaviors can make the immediate situation easier to live with, they ultimately serve to enable the alcoholic's drinking behavior. The family is conspiring with the alcoholic to deny and ignore the problem. In so doing, they line up to protect the family and prohibit outside intervention.

Certain factors contribute to a family's ability to deny the reality of alcoholism. Clearly, the degree and severity of drinking will affect the alcoholic's ability to parent and function within the home and on the job. The effects on the family facing economic disaster, eviction, or constant police intervention are different than for the family where alcoholism never becomes visible outside the home. However, and this is important to remember, the effects of drinking on the children in either family are equally devastating. It can be tempting to ignore the effects of parental alcoholism by comforting oneself with the notion, It wasn't that bad. But in either case, children are made to mistrust their perceptions because the family will not affirm them. Deep seeds of doubt, self-denial, and fear are planted in all of the children from these families.

Another confounding variable within the alcoholic family is the nondrinking parent's protectiveness. In an effort to keep the family together, these parents may distort reality by deliberately withholding information, even to the extent of rearranging memories in an attempt to shield themselves and their children from the pain and reality of alcoholism. Such "protective" behavior denies children the opportunity for creative conflict resolution. It also reinforces the family denial system and protects the alcoholic from having to take any responsibility for his or her behavior. A further result of the overprotectiveness of some nonalcoholic parents is that it fills children with vague fears. I have seen myself and many other ACOAs describe the phenomenon of imagining negative outcomes before fully entertaining any new ideas. Constant disappointment and unmet expectations leave an ACOA expecting the worst. It's like cement boots that we can't leave at home. John put it this way: "I would do well and be glad, but I still have this fear. It's scary, either I will succeed or I will fail, and either one is a problem. If I succeed, it won't be good enough, and if I fail, it's wrong.'' Attitudes like this, which were instilled in childhood, will make the process of recovery very difficult, but not impossible. Recovery requires that you become familiar with your own internalized adaptations, followed by relearning that the world can be a dependable place in which to make plans that can actually happen, and that you can make mistakes and the world will not end.

As the code of denial begins to drop, the family can move into a second stage of reaction to alcoholism. Individual family members become less passive; alcoholism is identified and named. Family members turn their attention onto themselves rather than staying focused on the alcoholic. This stage of family reaction requires overcoming the significant taboo of denial that characteristically surrounds the alcoholic family and recognizing the availability of help outside the home. Individual family members can become more aware of the problems caused by alcoholism and can attend to an intuitive need to ''feel normal.''

A third stage of reaction begins when a family confronts the possibility of separation as the only means for survival. Family members withdraw from one another, sometimes polarizing into factions or ''taking sides.'' Impending divorce adds more confusion, fear, anger, and isolation. Younger children may be left feeling abandoned, while older children feel relief.

The individual personality style of an alcoholic will affect family members' reactions to alcoholism. An abusive, loud, argumentative drunk will inspire different adaptive behaviors from the family than will a passive, negligent one. Generally, children have the ability to differentiate a person from his or her behavior. But as the disease of alcoholism progresses, the kinds of behavior a child is asked to understand will also change. Here the child's ability to accept and understand may become overtaxed.

The final stage of family reaction is family unity, which, sadly, many families never reach. The central issue at this stage is the alcoholic's sobriety, but that in itself may not be enough. The entire family's long-denied expectations need to be expressed, examined, refashioned, and clearly agreed upon because the damage suffered by the family during the preceding stages requires more than sobriety for repair.

Can you see your family in any of these stages? Can you tell where you got stuck or where the process of reacting stopped? Is your family still in process with the alcoholic? Are you?

There are a growing number of support and therapy groups for COAs and ACOAs, even grandchildren of alcoholics, as well as many excellent books, so if your family is not doing any work around the issues of alcoholism, it is still possible for you to learn and change and start to feel better. One word of warning as you begin the process of recovery: Do not expect your family to be supportive and understanding if they still have an investment in denying the reality of alcoholism.

I have sketched a general family backdrop for the

stage on which the drama of family alcoholism is played out. It is now time to watch how individual family members act out their roles of survival.

The primary reason for the formation of adaptive behaviors in COAs is parental role inconsistency, demonstrated by both the drinking and nonalcoholic parent. The drinking parent will fulfill his or her role quite differently depending on the blood-alcohol level in his or her system. Behavior will vary depending on if the alcoholic is feeling drunk, hung over, guilty about the last drinking binge, angry, or stressed. Out of necessity, children develop wide radar screens for detecting which mood they're likely to encounter. At the same time they devise intricate ways to try to get their own needs met. They learn to suppress their needs or to adapt their behaviors around the inconsistency of the parent. The nonalcoholic parent's behavior may also be inconsistent depending on whether he or she is reacting to, protecting, or arguing with the alcoholic.

During a single day a child may have to make several adaptations; for example, be the "parent" in the morning, getting breakfast for younger siblings; be a high school student all day; and then be the verbally abused, "good for nothing" child all evening. As with children in other troubled family situations, those in alcoholic homes develop roles to try to secure some sense of control in their lives. Sharon Wegscheider-Cruse and Claudia Black have described various coping roles in their work. It is important to keep in mind that these roles are not mutually exclusive, nor are they birth-order dependent as was once thought. Each role is dependent upon the environment within which the COA grew, and that COA's perceptions of his or her environment. All COAs and ACOAs probably have parts of each of these adaptive roles within them as a result of the constant challenge to adjust to the conflicting parental messages:

"I'm your parent. . . . Take care of me.

You can't do anything right. . . . I need you.

Everything is fine. . . . Don't worry.

Nothing is wrong. . . . Don't tell anyone."

One common role adaptation is that of "Hero" or "Responsible Child." These children exhibit high levels of responsibility, leadership, and maturity. If you ask a "Hero" about his or her childhood, the answer will most likely be, "I didn't have one." This adaptation, while it is highly valued by the adult world, robs children of the ability to experience childhood.

Another child may choose to act out in order to secure attention from the adult world. This is the "Acting Out" or "Scapegoat" role. Frequently these children will get into trouble with drugs and/or alcohol themselves. They are filled with feelings of rage and low self-esteem. Ironically, it is usually these COAs who get recognized as needing help from outside the home while most other COAs go unnoticed and untreated.

A third adaptation is the "Lost Child" or "Adjuster,"

the passive, withdrawn child who stays flexible by avoiding all responsibility. This child causes no problems and he or she is loved for that. Such children grow into adulthood without a sense of direction, and no sense of personal power or choice. The role is rewarded within the family because no attention, either positive or negative, is brought to it. But the adult child may find him or herself severely limited by this passive, adapting behavior style.

Then there is the child who decides to draw attention away from the imperfections of the family; the ultimate camouflage. This is the "Family Mascot" or "Clown." Insidiously, this is the child that appears to be "untouched" by family alcoholism.

Some children will take on the role of family social worker, "Placater," trying to rescue everyone while completely ignoring their own needs. Again, this role is valued by the adult world and generally goes unrecognized as a sign of trouble.

In general, all of these roles require children to curb their feelings and physical behavior—to grow up too fast. These children learn to anticipate adult reactions which, in turn, limits their own childishness. Parents and society see only competent, capable child-adults and ignore the costs being paid for this maturity.

Now you are probably wondering, "What role did I play? What role am I still playng?" As I said, most COAs and ACOAs have parts of all the adaptive roles inside them. When I interviewed ACOAs, one of the questions that I asked, which can provide many clues to your own adaptive role, was to complete the sentence:

What Went On In There?

*   *   *

"I was the one in the family who always _____."
Some of the answers were:

"ran and hid."

"tried to take care of everything."

"knew all of the family secrets."

"went to my room."

"thought I knew what was going on."

"was expected to be responsible."

"expressed everyone else's emotions."

"ran out."

One of the most damaging aspects of the various role adaptations is that each one causes children to struggle to hide and deny their own feelings of vulnerability and to doubt their true selves. Two major aspects of healthy personality development are the ability to discriminate fear from fact, and the ability to confirm one's perceptions with reality. Once children can make the distinction they can both defend against danger and open themselves fearlessly to others. They can risk vulnerability. Fear and fact, however, can easily become confused for COAs who witness strange, erratic behavior which is not explained and often seems to be ignored by the rest of the family. For these children, life is too unpredictable to let down defenses for one moment. The result is the development of self-doubt and an inability to risk vulnerability. Jenny described those feelings to me this way:

This caused a lot of anxiety and fear. A lot of confusion. On one level I understood and on another I really didn't. I didn't have the emotional depth to cope with what I understood. So I felt scared and very distrustful of other people. There was no one to talk to.

The self-rejection experienced by COAs leaves them feeling powerless. Their problems are not seen as opportunities, and they can't be made to go away, so COAs fall back onto the family model of denial and repression. They turn off feelings they cannot bear to encounter. Under the guise of self-protection, these coping mechanisms numb and further paralyze the child. COAs cannot protect themselves from threats they refuse (or are not allowed) to see, and they cannot meet the needs that they refuse to feel.

Defenses are protective devices. They help keep stress at manageable levels if they are flexible and adaptive to new situations. It is when defenses become rigid and automatic, as they do for COAs, that they become hindrances and limits to a full experience of the world. Defenses become the only choice for children whose world is distorted by family alcoholism.

Without some form of intervention, the self-perception adopted by COAs will not go away for adult children. The outward activities of the adult child may be different, but inside nothing has changed. The absence of security, bred in childhood, has grown up to produce undesirable, even destructive, defense mechanisms in the adult.

There's a
Nightmare
In My Closet

I SPOTTED A CHILDREN'S BOOK RECENTLY CALLED *There's a Nightmare in My Closet* and I thought, "Ha, in mine too!" In the story, a young boy is frightened by a monster that sneaks out of his closet at night when the lights are turned out. One night the boy confronts the monster and scares it. Symbolically the boy overcomes his fear when he is able to see it in a form over which he has some power.

So, what if, as a child, you lived with such a monster? What if there was a monster in the living room, the kitchen, your parents' room, and in the hall? What if everything looked perfectly normal and no one who came into your house ever suspected the monster? And what if no one in your family would recognize or talk about the monster either, even though you were pretty sure they knew about it?

15

If no one could or would see the monster, you probably came to doubt your own perceptions. You might have thought you made it all up, and that the nightmare was somehow all your fault. You gave up trying to talk to anyone about it, and you sank back into your fear and your doubts. As hard as you tried to push the fear back, like everyone else around you seemed to be able to do, it just kept popping out. The harder you pushed, the more it popped out, and the fear would never take a form that you could recognize or understand, so you remained defenseless before it.

Years later, you are living your adult life and you keep hearing the rumbling of the monster, you catch sight of it out of the corner of your eye. It has followed you from high school, through college, and now here it is in your own home. It whispers, nagging, "What if? What if? What if?" The voice leaves you shaking every time you're considering doing something new, taking a risk, or making a change. Maybe you have found that the monster backs off or the voice gets softer if you add a little vodka to your orange juice in the morning or if you push it away with lots of food. Or maybe you just never slow down enough for the monster to find you. Between work and exercise, taking care of the family, there just isn't time for anything unexpected to sneak up and scare you. You have your fear under control, and you are keeping the monster at bay. You've scheduled your life so that it will not be as unpredictable and confusing as your childhood.

Now you can probably recognize the monster as being the alcoholism that existed in your family. Because this monster was not acknowledged or talked about as you grew up, you could never confront it or overcome your fears. You couldn't make your fear take a shape that you could face and survive. You brought into adulthood all of the fear and anxiety that you felt but could not name as a child. But now it is possible to face those fears and stop reacting to them or being controlled by them.

Normally, a small child overcomes anxieties with the help of parents or with stories that assure that everything will turn out fine in the end. But alcoholic parent(s) are unable to provide such reassurances. It takes a very resourceful child or the help of a perceptive outsider to provide any measure of safety for these kids.

Consider Karen, who instinctively knew that the way to escape the dread she felt in her own house where her parents fought constantly was to climb up into the neighbor's tree house and lose herself in daydreams and books. The neighbors recognized her need for escape and would feign ignorance of her whereabouts when her mother would call, screaming for her daughter. Or take Margaret, who asked her mother to read *The Three Billy Goats Gruff* to her every night before bed. Margaret unconsciously connected the troll, who hid menacingly under the bridge, to her own anxiety, and she could fall asleep with ease when she had been assured, by the symbol of the goat's eventual success at passage, that she too would get over the bridge unharmed. Literally, Margaret had devised a way to put her fear to sleep.

Sometimes the strategies that children develop to cope with their feelings will backfire. Like me, Brian started writing comic strips for other children who he suspected might have some of the same confusion he was feeling.

17

He hid the strips in his room so that no one would know what he was doing, or how strange he felt. His mother found them one day, recognized the similarities to their own family, and scolded the boy harshly. By trying to sort out his negative emotions in a concrete form, Brian had violated the taboo of the alcoholic family: DON'T TALK. His mother had reacted as if he had been telling family secrets outside the home. So Brian's method of coping and adjusting was wrenched out of his hands. He was left defenseless, and he began to withdraw.

Chances are that because alcoholism was never openly discussed in your home, neither was much attention given to your feelings of fear. You may have had to hide them, and you may have done that so well that no one even suspected that you were feeling anything at all.

Defiance is one common way that children who are feeling powerless will act out their frustrations and try to get someone to notice them. Therefore, certain behaviors may go ignored as manifestations of anxiety. Defiance can take both overt and covert forms. I believe the covert acts to be more hazardous, as they require a shifting of needs and emotions within the child in order to mask or obliterate his or her vulnerability.

Nancy, an adult child of an alcoholic mother, told me during our interview that as a child she had found the unpredictability within her home unbearable. She never knew if her mother would be nice or mean, would hug, punish, or ignore her when she came home from school. It made her feel very nervous to never know what she would find when she opened the front door. Eventually Nancy's anxiety became so intense that she felt she had nowhere to turn, no one to talk to who wouldn't just try to talk her out of her feelings. So, rather than honestly expressing her emotions—something she has never seen successfully modeled—Nancy decided to put all of her efforts into "not feeling at all." She became determined and focused on numbing her feelings, and burying her vulnerability. She saw that as her only hope for survival and escape. Much like the technique of creative visualization that will be discussed later in this book, Nancy conjured a visual image to help her accomplish her goal. She imagined applying asphalt over her feelings, which she saw as lying along her spine. She hoped that if she could just cover her feelings up with enough of the impermeable black material, nothing painful or unexpected would be able to pop up. She also hoped that the asphalt would provide protection from outside invasion, hurt, and disappointment. In short, she wanted nothing to be able to get into or out of her heart. For months she visualized the image of layer upon layer of asphalt being laid over her feelings until her emotions felt less raw, less sensitive. She felt she had succeeded in eradicating her feelings, but at what a cost? She buried the joy along with the pain.

Fortunately for Nancy, because she remembered the conscious imagery of paving her emotions as a child, she already had an image to work with when she entered therapy as an adult. When she was first asked about her feelings, she answered her therapist, "I don't know very much about my feelings, I buried them. But now I want to get them out. There have been a few things that grew up through the cracks, but I want to get out the jackhammers and get this stuff off. I'm tired of not being able to let anything touch my heart. I feel heavy and stiff. I want the asphalt off.''

Another form of adaptation for a child in an alcoholic family is to strive for control in order to escape the chaos. Specifically, this control can take simple or more destructive forms. When Brian was punished for writing his comic strips, he was left temporarily without a means of coping. The time he once spent in his room, working on the comics, was now empty and quite stressful. He felt a great need to get involved with something else within the safety of that room, to lessen the stress. The next activity that he picked went unnoticed and unpunished by his parents. It literally provided the order that he was craving. The walls of Brian's room were lined with bookshelves. He decided to catalog, card, cross-reference, and shelve all the books according to size and color. With absolutely no information of library science, Brian proceeded to organize and reorganize the books for months. He even devised an intricate system for checking books out from the library that no one visited. The exercise of ordering and the attendant fantasy of control provided Brian with a sense of mastery and an inviolate escape from anxiety.

Alicia told me that even now, as an adult with her own house, she gets uncomfortable and nervous unless all the papers, books, and magazines that sit on the tables are put into neat piles of diminishing size. She cannot tolerate clutter. Her living room looks like a tidy display case. As a child, she had retreated to her room and ''put things in order'' whenever the situation downstairs made her feel too anxious or scared. While we spoke, I absentmindedly moved an ashtray. Her hand immediately and automatically reached out to return it to its exact and correct spot on the table.

When he was very young, William used to hold food in his mouth. He would push it up along his gums, adding more with each meal. This act of defiance culminated each day with a scene. His mother and father would take him into his bathroom and stand over him, coaxing him to spit the food out into the toilet before he went to bed. Interestingly, this scene took place every evening during the ''cocktail hour.'' William's behavior did bring him a great deal of attention, which felt like power and control to the small boy. He had managed to ensure the direct attention of both parents for fifteen minutes each night before bedtime.

Another example is Mandy. She desperately wanted and needed the love and attention of her parents. In her attempt to secure that attention, she vowed that she would do everything they expected of her, even though she wasn't always clear about what that was. She studied hard and got A's in school, she competed and won in sports, and still her parents were so absorbed by alcoholism that they ignored her. They did not attend the ceremonies in which she was honored. So, in a desperate attempt to attract attention, she turned to self-mutilation. She viciously bit her fingernails until her fingertips were raw and bloody. Then she would pick or bite the nail beds until she had removed the nails all the way down to the cuticles. After a few months, this behavior became less painful. Her fingers, along with her emotions, got numb. The tragedy is that even this extreme action, this deliberate shout for help, went unnoticed. Her parents were somehow able to ignore her. The result was that Mandy was left feeling powerless, invisible, and lost. She grew to be an adult who denied her own needs and feelings in order to please others. She still craved the love and attention her parents had been unable to give her as a child. She had low self-esteem due to a lasting image she had of herself as an invisible child. She also had a lingering sense of impotence that forced her to constantly push herself to excel. To the world she appeared confident, competent and happy, while inside, she felt miserable and hopeless.

Rather than being able to let their childish, spontaneous actions exist, COAs are forced into a posture of reaction. This adaptation cuts children off from their intuitive, imaginative natures and cripples them as adults unless they are able to recapture some of the magic that was lost in childhood.

The strategies children devise to cope with their worlds are ingenious, but they may also be maladaptive to adult life. It is crucial that adult children look back and examine how they coped. Is it working now? If not, is there a more imaginative and satisfying way to try?

Child psychologists have long agreed upon the possible curative properties of play and fantasy. Since play may have been curtailed or aborted completely for a child struggling to survive in an alcoholic home, relearning to play can provide the possibility for overcoming the fears and resentment that ACOAs still carry. Adult children are no longer helpless children with limited resources. We can now safely overcome the fears that made us feel helpless and afraid as children.

I believe that the tools with which a child instinctively approaches and attempts to make sense of his or her world carry great importance and potential throughout life. I also believe that how a parent responds or reacts to a child's coping strategy will deeply influence the success or failure of that child's ability to cope in adult life. I think that imagination and creative play during childhood are important indicators of coping mechanisms. I believe that fantasy, play, and imagery carry great potential for healing. Many people, including ACOAs, have experienced receiving information in symbolic form, images and dreams, flashes of insight that make new information accessible, or shed new light.

For most ACOAs there are powerful images remaining from childhood that are not healthy. These images keep ACOAs stuck in negative self-concepts and destructive behaviors. I believe that such imagery, if identified and investigated, can be redesigned and used toward creating happier, healthier futures. Even if you grew up in a family that silenced you, or caused you to grow up too fast, that confused you or ignored you, it is possible to get out from under the influence.

During our interview, I asked Karen how she felt her parents had influenced her adult life. She thought a long time before answering:

One very specific way that I feel my parents have influenced my adult life is that I recognized sometime this year that my parents' incessant arguing, which was part

23

of their drinking pattern, had been incorporated into myself, my internal voices. I realized that I was carrying their arguing inside of me. I had patterned my internal dialogue after theirs. One side of it was a weak, passive-aggressive person like my dad. One side was abrasive, bitchy, aggressive, and never satisfied. That side was always picking, picking, picking. That was my mom. That was the internal side of my own dialogue until one day I said, "Why don't you give them the divorce you always dreamed of?" I saw that I didn't have to keep up the same argument I had heard all my life. It was a very freeing realization to have, first to see that I was still carrying them around with me, and then to see that I was no longer powerless and paralyzed. I could finally give them the divorce I had imagined as a child. I have done some visualization around this and have managed to change the quality of my internal experience.

I believe that the level of creativity an individual can bring to bear on the attempt to cope is significant. Someone who cannot allow his or her own creativity to be playful, or who denies any creative potential, will remain stuck as a helpless victim. At the same time, until a fear can be experienced as manageable, rather than life threatening, as it may once have felt, we cannot be moved toward the possibility of change. Fear will paralyze creativity.

The process of recovery involves identifying and understanding what happened to you as a child. This is the "finding-and-naming-and-knowing-what-the-monster-looks-like" part. This may also be where you begin to identify the role you played in the family. It is important to understand how you survived the chaos of family alcoholism. The next step, as an adult, is to decide what to do about the shadows that remain in your present life as a result of your past.

PART TWO

Stop,
Look and
Listen

I WAS WRITING A LIST OF MY DREAMS AND WISHES IN my journal one day, an exercise that I followed by listing all of the concerns that stood between me and the actualization of my desires. I had spent maybe an hour on the exercise before I stepped back to take a look at what I had written. There it was, inescapably clear. Every single one of my concerns started with the phrase, "I'm afraid . . ." The problem was clear—how to get over my fears and to get out of my own way? It seemed that the process would involve putting aside the rules and assumptions I had always used, and setting off into unexplored territory.

The trick for ACOAs is to also ensure a level of security that will make exploring an act of free curiosity rather than imposed will. For the child who was never given permission to feel his or her feelings based on the actual situation, such a level of security must be designed and achieved. Constant doubt in one's perceptions will dampen any ACOA's imaginative abilities. Efforts like writing, drawing, and daydreaming, which were punished or denied during childhood, need to be brought out again and reexperienced as permissible.

Jenny spoke of it this way:

I have just started trying to remember my childhood. There is a lot I don't remember; they are just blank years. It's really like what you are talking about with creativity. I mean, there just wasn't enough room to be alive, to be myself. To stand up for myself or express an opinion. That is the strongest sense I have, the fear of making the wrong move. So, I think, just to express myself brought up the most fear.

Until the fifth grade I really drew a lot. I was very good at drawing. I don't know what happened between fourth and fifth grades, but something seriously shifted. I feel a very strong block. I find it difficult to sit down and draw. As I start getting back to drawing now, it is hard for me to sit down and really do anything. It's hard to make myself calm enough to sit still. I start getting scared. Most anytime I start doing anything I really want to do, there is this whole sense of having to start looking around.

I also get hooked into controlling, to thinking that I have to have a certain space and amount of time. "This won't work, but this has to be." And if I can't get that, then I have to wait. If I don't have the right pen, or the perfect drawing table, I'll start and then not be able to hold my attention to it. It's like it no longer exists. I cannot access it as soon as I start to pay attention to it. Fear comes up for me, but I also feel compelled to express myself a lot, but as soon as I start doing it in one area then I just totally diminish its quality and its importance.

If a child is forced to express the content of his or her unconscious mind, the natural resource of fantasy will become limited, leaving the child with diminished ability to face the struggles of life. Fear replaces curiosity; comfort replaces creativity. My hope is that it's never too late to reacquaint ourselves with imagination and to move fear to the side for the sake of self-expression and optimistic fantasy.

ACOAs describe the feeling of "being stuck," of believing that the choices they are making will be different while finding that nothing has changed. Feeling stuck is when you believe that your options are limited, that there are no alternatives to the way things are. Fear of uncertainty and the conflict that arises with change will further contribute to immobilization. Creativity involves looking for change, breaking habitual ways of thinking and getting unstuck. Creativity means openness and receptivity, not fear and paralysis.

Creative expression requires courage. Fear and anxiety are necessary parts of the process as well. Courage is not the absence of despair, but rather the capacity to move ahead in spite of it, a trusting that will not be squashed by fear. This is a crucial idea for ACOAs to remember, as trusting in the face of despair is commonly quite painful, if not impossible. The unconscious mind can sometimes present us with that which is most threatening, forcing us to hold more tightly to our conscious thinking and need for control.

Dreams and insights represent the dynamic struggle between tightly held ideas and beliefs. They can bring anxiety and guilt as well as joy and the actualization of a new vision. Guilt is also a sharply felt emotion for any ACOA, therefore, he or she might avoid following an insight that threatened a tightly held belief. Unconscious breakthroughs can be quite unsettling for ACOAs who have not made the decision to risk creative change.

Creative experience has a quality of absorption and intensity that can be overwhelming and scary for ACOAs whose sense of safety requires maintaining tight control of themselves. In short, ACOAs who are heavily invested in not changing—who would rather cling to rigid, dogmatic, previously made conclusions—will never allow themselves access to the knowledge that exists on another level. They will have completely adopted the parental stance that inhibited their adventure, creativity, and spontaneous play as a child.

There are ACOAs for whom remaining stuck in rigid, predictable patterns is unacceptable. These ACOAs refuse to continuously accept the boundaries of their heritage. These are adults who managed to maintain some optimistic glimmer from childhood. These are creative souls who can see anxiety as an opportunity for growth rather than as a threat. These are children from alcoholic families who preserved a healthy level of flexibility and openness that kept them receptive to their creative impulses.

I suspect there is a third group of people who are stuck somewhere in between openness and rigidity—people who are struggling to open their spirits and loosen the restrictions that were placed on their playfulness as children, people striving to redesign their lives for more satisfaction and fun. These people, and I include myself among them, are not at the stage of accepting anxiety as a challenge, but neither will they do anything actively to keep anxiety at bay. These people can accept anxiety and use it to mold their disorderly worlds into what they desire. One woman described herself to me this way:

I had little privacy. I had very little space of my own. Since I had no safe place, I withdrew into myself. Years and years of therapy are the only way I have found to get out, and mostly, more than therapy, there was a desire in me to live and to be alive inside. It's painful, but what other choice do you have? I know I don't want to be like them, and I can't be unconscious. So, I guess, I wanted to be healthy.

Edith saw herself this way:

One of the reasons that I waited so long to get married and to have a child was because I wanted to get free. Because I know that whenever faced with a stressful situation, you revert. You revert to whatever was done to you and whatever is in there, it's just what comes out.

An important distinction to keep in mind is that there are two types of anxiety. One is a feeling of apprehension that accompanies formative, creative, and expansive times. This is the anxiety of possibility and must remain grounded, or in balance, in order to be useful. Fritz Perls put it this way, ''Anxiety is ungrounded excitement.'' The second form of anxiety is neurotic, characterized by withdrawal, inhibition, and blocked vitality.

Clearly, fear, anxiety, and self-doubt are the major stumbling blocks to creativity in any individual. It is important for an ACOA to discover the manifestations, the internal voices, and the ''I'm afraid'' messages in order to begin the process of rediscovery and recovery. Internal voices can be changed to more accurately suit the adult. This in itself is an act of creation. As Rollo May states, ''The creative act arises out of a struggle of human beings with and against that which limits them.''

CREATIVITY IS ADULT PLAY

Childhood is an essential period of life to which everyone is entitled. It is the necessary foundation for adulthood. Children who grow up in alcoholic homes develop patterns of behavior and thought that minimize the pain and chaos and optimize safety. These children become emotional adults; they grow up too fast. Later in life, because they didn't have a chance to really be children, some ACOAs will find that they do not know how to play, how to be spontaneous. Personally, I found that my creativity and playfulness were blocked by frightful self-consciousness. I had taught myself how to act in a controlled way, and now I couldn't let go. The gradual return to playfulness and free creative expression has felt like an enormous step toward recovery and wholeness.

In a society that has become increasingly focused on production and accomplishment, we should all fear for the future of pure playfulness. As we speed ourselves up in the "search for excellence," we lose our sense of magic and abandon. I dread the loss of play not only because it signals the devaluation of fun for its own sake, but also because play, imagery, and creative endeavor provide people with important releases from stress.

Maria Montessori believed that play is the work done by children. I would add that creativity is adult play. Both serve the function of providing enjoyment while reducing internal stress. Listening to fairy tales and daydreaming help children understand the stresses of life by allowing the symbolic resolution of feelings and conflicts. Stories and play games stimulate and nurture a child's inner resources for coping by bringing together messages from the conscious, unconscious, and preconscious minds. As children begin to make sense out of the world around them, they feel less anxiety. Freud called this "Primary Process Thinking," a special mode of thought that gives rise to dreams, fantasy, jokes, and play. Through these modes of expression a person can vent needs and desires, especially those that are not approved by society. In short, play works like a safety valve, discharging socially unacceptable feelings, wishes, and desires through imaginative substitutes.

As children, we had very little influence over the situations of our daily lives. But as adults, we are responsible for creating our own reality. Our thoughts, feelings, and beliefs all influence the quality of our lives. As children, we may have learned that we were powerless to change much of the reality of our lives; so as adults, it can be a challenge to take full responsibility for creating the realities that we desire. ACOAs all carry a wounded child filled with fear, hurt, and anger. But there is also a child inside who is filled with wonder and magic. Both children need careful attention, acceptance, and love.

What do you think of when you think of playing? Can you remember yourself playing as a child? Do you think of being "out of control" or getting punished? Do you think you're "wasting time" or "being foolish"? Do you think you really "should" be doing something else, or not acting so "childish"?

If you think this way about playing, it really isn't any wonder because alcoholic parents who demand complete obedience from children might punish the normally integrative behaviors of play, fantasy, and creative expression with taunts like, "Don't be daydreaming all the time," or "You act like such a baby," or "You should be upstairs doing your homework." Such taunts will be internalized by children as they struggle for acceptance and love. In short, parents and children conspire to make feelings go away and children get separated from the imaginative thought process that provided soothing solutions to troubled feelings. The children lose the ability to externalize what is going on internally. They lose the spontaneous impulse for play. What is left is confusion and a need for tight self-control.

The dictionary tells us that to play is to be involved in

recreation: re-creation. I think of play as more of an attitude than as something to do. One can create an attitude of play even when engaging in the most serious of activities. An attitude of playfulness can make boring tasks fun and frightening jobs more exciting.

Transactional Analysis has given us the concepts of the Natural Child and the Adapted Child. The Natural Child is the spontaneous, fun-loving and mischievous part, while the Adapted Child depends on parental approval and will do anything to secure it. The Adapted Child performs, obeys, and works especially hard to incorporate conflicting parental messages in order to secure parental love. The emotional repression that exists in an alcoholic home forces children to become divided within themselves. The normal expression of impulses and emotions gets replaced by a stronger need to get approval. Is there any doubt that the alcoholic family system produces Adapted Children?

Learning to be playful again requires reacquainting ourselves with our Natural Child. Here are some characteristics of the Natural Child. Can you find any of them in yourself?

Likes to experiment.

Is fascinated by the environment.

Has free use of his or her imagination.

Imitates others, is not afraid to try new behaviors.

Is free to be silly or wrong.

37

Unfortunately, the Adapted Child has certain character-istics that directly challenge the Natural Child.

Needs a time schedule.

Is competitive.

Has to "do it right."

Is overly serious.

Has a strong sense of organization.

The Adapted Child is more likely to win the approval of parents. He or she speaks of, "I should, I could, I'll try," and gets positive reinforcement. The Natural Child, on the other hand, gets increasingly neglected and for-gotten. Relearning playfulness requires finding your Nat-ural Child again.

You might want to start by picking a role model, someone you know who seems comfortable with play, who can laugh at him or herself and who seems to truly enjoy him or herself and life without feeling guilty. Once you have chosen this role model, keep your eyes and ears open for evidence of his or her Natural Child.

Everyone needs role models in their lives. Someone to learn from, model oneself after, or simply to admire. But beware, ACOAs tend to pick someone to *become*. This is a denial of oneself as well as a setup for disappoint-ment. If my role model is up on a pedestal, it is probable that I will fall short of my expectation to be just like her. Therefore, it is healthier, when picking role models, to choose aspects of a model to emulate rather than one person to try to clone yourself after.

In the interviews I've conducted with ACOAs, I have clearly seen that many had important role models or stories that provided crucial assurances. Margo tells me of her childhood love for the stories of *Pippi Longstocking*, a book she used to read to herself continually. The connections are inescapable—Pippi Longstocking is a child who lives without grown-ups in her own house with a monkey, a horse, and a trunk full of gold pieces. She is fiercely independent, playful, and "naughty" by all adult standards. I look at Margo, a competent, single woman with a cat and a horse, living alone, having adventures. I see Pippi Longstocking very clearly as Margo and I sit across the table from one another.

Karen tells me of her compulsion to have her mother read and reread the story of Bambi to her. I puzzle for a moment before Karen adds, "Well, of course, I know what that was all about. My mother was giving me the same survival training that Bambi's mother gave about how to live in the forest. No wonder it gave me so much comfort to hear." I suspect it may have been about how to live without a mother as well.

Peg describes an image she used to have of herself as a horse. She would wrap a huge black cape around herself, disguising the little girl, and become a wild horse who could run off and escape anything that was going on around her.

Helen describes a lifelong fixation with Amelia Earhart. At age nine she discovered this mystery woman who provided a model for independence and movement that continues to fascinate and nourish her thirty years later.

Lucy described herself this way:

I've always wanted to know about other people, how they lived their lives, what they grew up and did. I was constantly, and still am, a role-model junkie. If I could just find someone that seemed to be doing it right and then fashion my life after theirs.

I believe that these role models and characters provide optimism and hope for the children and are, therefore, very important indicators of the need that children have for security, order, and safety. I believe that fantasy and creative visualization can serve the same purposes of projection and identification for an adult. However, by adulthood, many other censors may have sneaked in to confuse the messages. Internal censors are born out of criticism, lack of encouragement and punishment, and will cut an ACOA off from any message of comfort or self-awareness. The adult gets trapped in what Freud called "Secondary Process Thinking," which is characterized by rational, rule-regulated thought.

John put it this way:

I would say now that despite the fact that I do well at a lot of things, there is still a feeling of self-doubt, that I don't quite belong. So, I'm a fake in a sense. No matter how well I do, and even when I think I am doing well, I also feel like it's not really true. "I can't do that." It was never good enough, that's for sure. It's subconscious.

40

Stop, Look and Listen

All I know is that when I start heading in a direction that is going to be constructive and productive, it just takes a side track and ends. One time I got a little gap with that subconscious behavior and I saw it, and I started to watch it, and it was my mother, and I heard the voice.

Eddie added:

What is destructive for me is this condemning, driving thing that I have from my mother that just drives me to work. Nothing is ever good enough. I'll drive myself to the point of total exhaustion and then I will do whatever it is to an extent that I then react against it and don't want to do it anymore. This is a real destructive thing in me. My parents were very critical. I am just consumed with it, riddled with guilt.

On the flip side, there are some children who long for a sort of fusion with the parent. It seems that this desire is associated with the need to feel close to that drinking parent, which lessens the constant fear of abandonment.

Ruth explained it this way:

I remember driving around with my father one time when I was a teenager. I loved him very much, and I was always hungry for some proof that there was a special bond between us. I would settle for just about anything that I could take as a sign of his love for me. On this particular trip, I can remember it well, he told me that he felt close to me because we shared something. All I could hear was that he felt close to me, and I was flying.

41

He went on to explain the thing that we shared was our huge sense of guilt over everything. I never stopped for an instant to question his perception or to register that guilt was not exactly a desirable thing for us to share as a bond. Now it makes me sick to think of how much I wanted him to love me and not leave me, and how willing I was to accept anything, even a huge guilt complex, as proof.

The process of recovery for ACOAs requires going back to question and reexamine everything they learned in childhood, discovering all the internalized messages, all the behavioral adaptations, and ending the pattern of denial, followed by the act of voluntary suffering. Voluntary suffering involves facing and feeling all the buried pain, disappointment, and grief of childhood in order to build a happier, more complete adulthood. ACOAs who truly wish to stop feeling stuck, to stop feeling like a victim, and to stop reacting like a robot, must be willing to examine fearlessly, reveal the myths, and truly *feel* reality as it was.

I cannot say that the process of recovery is without pain, sadness, and fear. But I can say that it is rewarding and certainly worthwhile for anyone who has ever suspected that he or she was being held back by something that couldn't be seen, touched, or escaped. There is no one, correct way to approach this process, but courage, patience, and trust are required. It is not through perfection that one heals, but rather through one's acquaintance with pain.

I still find myself slipping back into that place where I like to think that someday they will wake up and recognize what a wonderful person I am, but I guess that is never going to happen, at least not the way I want it to. But I get scared when I tell myself I will never have the love I want from them and then I feel so alone.

When I began the work of self-examination through reading about alcoholism and children of alcoholism, I found myself tapping my foot impatiently asking, "All right already, I understand this now, but what am I supposed to do about it? How do I start to *feel* better?" Slowly I came to recognize my tendency to move directly into problem solving as one of the greatest barriers to personal change. I suspect that other ACOAs have the same tendency—to jump from intellectualization straight into ardent problem solving. So, what's missing?

What's missing is the acknowledgment of feelings. There is certainly a reason that feelings were shoved into a closet, but recovery requires cleaning out that very same closet.

The alcoholic family, like any family, is a system that develops through continuous interaction, a shared frame of reality. This frame becomes a filter through which individual members experience the world. Because the alcoholic family is trapped in a dependency supported by denial and suppression, any movement toward honesty by a member will result in an upheaval within the system. The alcoholic family is typically unskilled at negotiation, opting instead for the maintenance of predictability through isolation and the demand for loyalty from all family members. The fact remains, however, that parents who ask children to negate the past will incapacitate those children to accept the present. As ACOAs become aware of the present-day problems that resulted from their adaptations to parental drinking, their relationships within the family will also change.

At first you may identify yourself as an enabler. "I was the one who always tried to rescue him. I realize now that I was just helping him to keep on drinking." Or perhaps you felt responsible for the drinking, along with feeling hopeless and helpless to make it stop. A tricky switch can happen as you begin to emerge from the position of victim into a position of self-love and recovery. As you begin to shed the denial, the rest of the family may move to close ranks, putting you into the role of persecutor and themselves into the role of victim. A crucial lesson that can be learned in an alcoholic family is that no one can be rescued who doesn't believe that he or she is drowning. People change as they feel the need. Don't try to rescue your entire family as you make steps toward recovery; they must do the work for themselves, at their own pace. If they decide to remain in denial and dysfunction, you will be better off to let them stay there. It's not your fault if they do not want to face reality and get out from under the influence of family alcoholism.

Okay. So where are we? Self-examination, acknowledgment of feelings, and voluntary suffering. How to proceed? Are you feeling scared? Okay, if you answered "Yes," that is a good first step. The process *is* scary and you have acknowledged a fear that I suspect you have not often expressed before. There are a couple of guidelines to keep in mind as we start exploring in the closets of our past.

You were, in all probability, well rehearsed in the avoidance of conflict and confrontation within your family. It is necessary to drop this stance in order to approach the work that you will need to do. Ignoring problems and your feelings has brought you to the place where you are today, wanting to "feel" better. But that behavior cannot take you any further. A good way to check out if you're avoiding the truth is to listen to yourself. Repeated "Yes . . . but" answers are a good indicator that there is something you are refusing to see, accept, or believe.

It is also time to start accepting your responsibility for yourself and your feelings. Your parent(s) were poor teachers on this point, refusing to take the proper responsibility for their behavior. You heard excuses like, "It's not a problem." "He's just drunk, don't blame him." "She just forgot to pick you up at school, it's no big deal, you're home now." All of these messages reflect the refusal to accept alcoholism as a problem. If there is no problem, then nothing has to change. But if you continue to accept these excuses, you will remain a victim or a martyr: "They made me feel this way by drinking too much and neglecting me." This is a position of powerlessness.

Another barrier to accepting responsibility for mending your feelings and behavior is that you may have taken on so much of the responsibility within your own family at such a young age that you feel burned-out and unwilling to take on any more. You may be tempted to ask yourself, ''What good will it do anyway?''

When you can truly accept that you were not responsible for the parental drinking, or for making your parent(s) more loving, you will have more energy and love to direct toward yourself. If you can truthfully accept that people do the best that they are able, and then mourn for the inadequacy of your parent(s)'s ''best,'' you will be well on the way to accepting full responsibility for your own growth, happiness, and fulfillment.

It is necessary to place before yourself a clear image of the reality of your childhood, your family, and yourself. It is time to stop denying, distorting, and discounting what really went on as you were growing up. This step will probably stir deep feelings of guilt and disloyalty. Welcome to the voluntary suffering part. It is time to stop thinking in an ''If only . . .'' mode and to accept reality for what it was.

Confronting reality means confronting your defense mechanisms. Asking yourself, ''What role did I play in my family? Do I still play it? What is the payoff for playing this role?'' is a good place to begin. Then, depending on your answers, challenge yourself to stick with an ideal image that you set before yourself rather than buckling under to a family that warns, ''Don't rock the boat,'' or ''You don't want to upset your father.''

Finally, striving for some measure of flexibility will be useful. Rigid, automatic responses, which were patterned in childhood and insured survival, are not easily given up. Ideally, ACOAs can learn flexibility as their reality becomes rooted in the present instead of mired in the past. Buried emotions are brought to the surface, accepted, and integrated. Awareness of one's own needs and desires becomes apparent after years of suppression. This is recovery! Cindy put it this way: "I always knew what other people wanted and needed. I had a special kind of radar. But I never knew what I needed, and no one around me ever asked."

Letting go of previously held ideas and behaviors is not as easy as it sounds, even if they are destructive to you. We developed those ideas and behaviors in order to survive, so letting go will feel quite threatening. Amy explained it this way:

I'm really just beginning to realize how unavailable my parents were to me as a child. I get very depressed, and I try to get away from the realization because it hurts too much. But then, some days, I have enough strength to confront it, so I imagine myself as a little baby, reaching out for someone. I am crying hysterically and no one comes to soothe me. Within seconds, I really am crying. I guess that's mourning. I sure feel better inside when I have allowed those tears to come out.

An image that helps me is that the reawakening process is sort of like the time I had to run warm water over my fingers that had gotten a touch of frostbite. As the feeling began to come back into the frozen fingers it was quite painful. But within minutes my fingers were no longer numb, and I could use them again.

There are many traps besides the tendency to over-intellectualize and skip over feelings. Each person's journey toward recovery will be personal and very individual. Recognizing your own traps will be a personal discovery. Challenging the conformity that you fashioned in your youth will bring many painful memories to the surface, but it will also unearth hidden allies for the journey.

The following chapter is an account of my face-to-face meeting with my Adapted Child and some of the exercises I've tried to coax my Natural Child back out of exile.

The Life and
Times of
Little Miss Perfect

$\mathcal{S}$EVERAL YEARS AGO I DISCOVERED A PERSON INSIDE OF me whom I named Little Miss Perfect. She materialized one afternoon as I was writing furiously in my journal. I was struggling with myself, learning to set my own limits, experimenting with saying "no" to other people's requests. I began to hear a harsh internal voice, ranting at me for every small step toward self-assertion. "You're being selfish; all you ever think of is yourself."

"Who are you?" I shouted out loud. "You're in my way; who are you anyway?"

There she was, four years old, dressed in a green, smocked-front party dress, black patent-leather shoes, and white ankle socks. Her blond hair neatly tugged back off her scrubbed face in a tidy barrette. A serious, directed look froze on her four-year-old face. She stared me right in the eye. I knew her immediately, Little Miss Perfect.

For a moment I couldn't believe she was still inside me, calling the shots. I flashed back to the memory of the day she was born. My sister and I had been identically dressed because pictures were going to be taken. I had been admonished not to get dirty or to mess up my hair before the photographer arrived. Nervous energy filled my little primped body, and I struggled to suppress my giggly urges. At some point, I slipped into the downstairs bathroom. As I sat back onto the seat, as I was used to doing in the upstairs bathroom, I slid backward and landed up to my neck in water. First there was shock, which was quickly replaced by a strangling sense of shame and fear. The pictures would be ruined and I would be in terrible trouble for intentionally disobeying and messing up my dress. No one would believe it had been an accident.

The realization of how quickly I had stepped in to punish myself, before anyone else even knew what had happened, was quite a shock. Had Little Miss Perfect sprung to life in order to "keep me on track," to make every attempt to please my parents? I scanned my past for other places where this little tyrant had been in charge. I burst into tears as I quickly realized the breadth of her reign.

I decided that it was important to get to know Little Miss Perfect, and, if possible, to work out some sort of truce. After all, she is a part of *me*. I began to listen to her and to watch her behavior. By just giving her a name I had personified her and made it possible for her to assume a recognizable form with which I could communicate. As much as I disliked her and wished she would go away, I tried only to observe, not to judge and condemn. In fact, there were places I found where Little Miss Perfect had been an asset. She had clearly served some good purposes for me.

Little Miss Perfect had been born out of my own attempts at survival within an alcoholic home. Through her I could begin to break some of the patterns of conceptualization that I had set up as a child. I had turned off switches to my own awareness without ever having noticed that I had done so. Now I am working toward controlling those switches with an internal rheostat. This way I can regulate the degree of awareness and inhibit the bombardment of stimuli. I can now experience a wide range of sensory awareness instead of living in an either/or mode of hypersensitivity or complete shutdown.

So, while ACOAs turn off their senses in order to survive the turmoil, as adults that survival is short-lived; too much else has been excluded in the process of shutting down sensory and emotional awareness.

At the same time that I was getting acquainted with Little Miss Perfect, I read a powerful book, *The Drama of the Gifted Child*, by Alice Miller. She introduced me to the concept of narcissistic parents, parents who are so insecure and needy themselves that they inadvertently force their own children to fulfill their conscious and unconscious needs. These parents cannot permit or attend to the neediness of their children because to do so would be too threatening. Suddenly, I had a context within which to look at the nagging voice inside of myself who always asked, "What about me? Why can't I have what I want *too*?" For the first time I could see where the "You are selfish" messages had come from. My parents were too needy themselves to let go of much. Once I saw this, forgiving them and forgiving myself was easier.

Alice Miller describes narcissistic parents as being able to see the "goodness" of their children only if it reflects back onto themselves. Moves toward autonomy by the child are perceived as threats. These were the parents that Little Miss Perfect had come to serve.

Miller points out the likelihood that narcissistic parents had childhoods that were also darkened by narcissistic parents, causing them to bring their neglected childhood needs to bear on the next generation. Here was another family legacy that passed from generation to generation like alcoholism.

Parents who cannot see and appreciate their children as separate, independent individuals miss seeing the uniqueness of each child. To prevent feeling threatened, parents may blame or even punish children for having dreams and wishes of their own. Common taunts include, "You're such a selfish, unthankful kid." Or, "Don't you ever think of anybody but yourself?" Or, "You're just doing that to make me mad, now stop it." Understandably, children raised by such parents will fail to learn about spontaneous sharing and giving. They will not see such behavior modeled at home, and they may be punished for outbursts of their own. These children will learn to deny their pleasure and strive for altruism and perfection in order to secure parental approval and lessen anxieties about being punished or abandoned.

Mandy was just beginning to examine her childhood in recovery when we interviewed. She told me:

Part of being an ACOA for me means that I have to work extra hard to please everybody. Somehow I have to go back and recapture parts of my life from my parents in order to feel like a complete person. This reexamination has wiped away a lot of my ability to continue to forgive or deny behavior that had always been hurtful. I suddenly stood face-to-face with lots of neglect that I had tried desperately not to see. . . . I mean, my parents think I hate them now because I am in therapy trying to get some help. How narcissistic can you get? It's like with both of my parents, their needs dwarf mine. It has always been that way. I can never get anything without them seeing it as their loss.

When I asked Eddie what had seemed most forbidden to her as a child, she answered:

I guess it was something to do with my not performing well in social situations. Not meeting my mother's expectations, that sort of thing. It was forbidden to not be presentable. I used to have a journal, and I wrote in it every day for many years. I can't remember the phrase that I had for it . . . but it's like being an extension of my mother's social front. It didn't matter what was going on, or how you felt, or what was appropriate in terms of human reality, all that mattered was what the appearance was.

I propose that alcoholic parents are the quintessential narcissistic parents. Their self-absorption and the disease of alcoholism obliterate the possibility of perceiving the needs of others. Their own feelings and needs were ignored, and now they are drowned with alcohol. Quite literally, their vision is blurred by their addiction. The nonalcoholic spouse may not have sufficient energy to direct toward the children either. By insisting upon respect, obedience and love, these narcissistic parents train their children, basically, to be their own parents. The children, in turn, get separated from their true childselves and turn into parental please-machines, conforming to the parents and denying themselves. COAs get so oversensitized to their parents' needs that they cease to attend to, or even recognize, their own.

Clearly such parenting styles force children to grow up too fast. By prohibiting childishness, in favor of conformity, achievement and perfection, parents do not allow their kids to be kids. They push them prematurely into adulthood. These kids are trying to cope while also hiding their confusion. They get cut off too early from their fantasy lives, which allow for the healthy integration and understanding of common feelings. Children who have been hurried into adulthood cannot stand back from themselves; they cannot escape into fantasy and play. They are ever-mindful of everyone but themselves. They fail to develop the inner resources that allow for the integration and mutual support of emotions, intellect, and imagination. These children are quite serious and get little relief from their constant self-criticism and anxiety.

When I asked Karen about her fantasy life as a child, she told me:

I think I did have an active fantasy life. It feels also to me like I was riveted on reality. Reading gave me structured fantasy and was the escape place for me. I would get totally absorbed in that rather than more active, wilder fantasy. I wouldn't go there. It was sort of like I had to be "on call," that was the tense part. At any moment, if I were too far out, when the beeper went off I wouldn't be able to get back. I think also that the concept of a fantasy world probably made me feel vulnerable. The times I would go off would be scary.

Feelings and emotions have their own timing and cannot be hurried or slowed down to suit the sensibilities of others. The hurried child pays a terrible price. My own Little Miss Perfect may have secured my survival, but she certainly forfeited a lot of playfulness and fun. She had learned how to read minds and to do whatever was expected, but she was grossly deficient in her ability to do anything for me, the child she had, in fact, replaced. Unchallenged, my Adapted Child was strangling my Natural Child.

Children who adopt adult-like coping personalities still *feel* like children. They still have childish emotions, impulses, dreams, and fears despite their valiant efforts at eradication or camouflage. Alcoholic parent(s) and other adults do not make the distinction. They make the incorrect assumption that children who act as if they understand mature issues actually do. COAs will do their best to hide their confusion and childishness, but repeated exposure to adult matters, and warnings to understand and accept them, will not necessarily produce the ability to do so. The task of self-discovery is made more difficult for children who are presented with the problems and difficulties of others before they have had sufficient chance to find some order and meaning in their own lives.

There is another hidden danger. Kids who strive for perfection and parental approval are admired by adults, parents, and teachers. Such children look successful while feeling empty, depressed, and alienated. Their pain becomes invisible, though they are often plagued by unrecognized anxiety, guilt, and shame. There is a constant internal pressure to live up to their image of themselves. My own Little Miss Perfect worked overtime to ensure nothing less than perfection. She got As in school, had all homework done on time, and sent prompt thank-you notes. But in her efforts to preserve the image of success that guaranteed her survival, she locked my true child-self, my Natural Child, in a closet. Consequently, my autonomy was limited and the developmental process of individuation was prevented. Once I discovered this as an adult, it was time to review her job description and make some adjustments.

As children develop, they are actively involved with constructing their personal reality out of experiences and the surrounding environment. As children progress, the content and form of their thought process will change.

But, if they are stymied at a particular stage of development, each progressive stage will show distortion. Normally, infants who experience the world as a dependable place, a place where their needs are met on time and in a consistent fashion, will acquire a sense of trust that extends beyond their immediate caretakers. However, COAs rarely get such timely, consistent care. Their sense of trust and the ability to extend that trust to others becomes severely limited. Instead of learning to be open, accepting and trusting, these children learn to steel themselves against fear, neglect, and abandonment. They guard themselves against vulnerability, the dreaded "V-word," at all times. Furthermore, these same children may be expected to take on the caretaking function of the parent. Unfortunately, these parent-children also adopt many of the critical, scolding voices of their parent(s). Little Miss Perfect may have protected me in certain areas, but she was also a relentless, pushy, and highly critical internal driver.

In order to establish healthy levels of initiative and self-assertion, all children need time to explore within a safe and responsive environment. Alcoholic households typically fail to provide such nurturing environments, leaving children to scavenge safety and attention where they can or learn to do without. Normally, daydreaming, playing, and fantasizing within a supportive environment are the ways children come to express, understand, and live with their fears. Without the involvement and help of caring parents, the imaginative strategies will be of little use. The children are left with only their undeveloped intellectual powers of reasoning as a resource. They

57

struggle to apply adult tools to childhood problems. Parents can further increase children's anxiety with messages like, "Don't be so childish. Don't always be daydreaming off in some cloud." Or, the worst message of all, "You just have to understand it, that's the way adults are. He or she didn't mean it; he or she has had too much to drink." In every instance the children's feelings remain completely unattended, while the abusive behavior of the parents is mysteriously justified.

Even if we are not actively talking with another person, each and every one of us is carrying on a conversation with ourselves. You may or may not be aware of your internal conversation, but it will direct the way you view the world and yourself. And this internal conversation is vulnerable to the same distortions and misunderstandings as any other conversation.

The phenomenon of talking to ourselves is related to self-awareness. It includes our intuition, dreams, fantasies, and coping strategies as well as our attunement with our bodies, emotions, wishes, and needs. We describe and evaluate the world to ourselves, and we talk to ourselves about ourselves. Most of our self-concept and our feelings of self-worth depend on what and how we talk to ourselves in these intrapersonal conversations. Listen to yourself as you go through the day. Are you scolding or ridiculing yourself? Or are you encouraging and praising yourself? It will make a difference in the way you feel and in the way you act.

Children in an alcoholic home hear many confusing, if not outwardly critical, messages from the outside world. They take them in without question, and begin delivering the same message internally. These internalized messages add up to crush a once healthy self-concept, and to create a fearful, lonely, and unnourishing internal environment. Without help, nothing changes for grown children as they become adults. The internal environment will remain a hostile territory.

Can you close your eyes and hear any of the parental taunts that you used to hear when you were a child? Who is delivering those messages these days? Have you, in fact, taken over the role of providing yourself with those same messages? Can you see or hear your Adapted Child? Can you think of a way to coax your Natural Child out of hiding? How do these two different aspects of yourself, the Adapted Child and the Natural Child, respond to your internal dialogue? Who talks the loudest?

Now that you can hear them clearly, do you really want to continue giving yourself those messages? Or are you tired of hearing all of that criticism? If you don't want to hear it anymore, can you think of ways to stop the voices?

You might want to try imagining a conversation, or negotiation between your Natural Child and your Adapted Child, or between any of the other internal voices. Be careful here, this is not a time to condemn or judge, or attempt to banish any parts of yourself, no matter how unacceptable they may appear to you. This is a time for recognizing, accepting, and working out a truce with yourself. This is a time to forgive yourself and to love yourself, all parts of yourself.

In recovery, as we begin to realize that despite the

damage, we had our particular set of parents for a reason, we can begin to stop blaming them and begin to move onward. When we can accept alcoholism as a disease, we no longer have to blame anyone, and most importantly, we can stop blaming ourselves. We can stop feeling like defenseless victims as we begin assuming the responsibility for our own growth and letting go of our false sense of responsibility for the drinking behavior of our parent(s). This process requires learning about the disease of alcoholism and the effects it had on us as children. It also requires adopting a trust in ourselves and in our feelings that may have to begin as a pure leap of faith until it becomes more familiar. As resourceful adults, we have the power to manifest either a positive or a negative reality for ourselves. We are not helpless children anymore. It is up to us to decide that we are responsible for our present-day reality and then go about fashioning it to our liking.

Are you trembling at the thought? It is an exhilarating idea, but it takes some getting used to. Perhaps we should take another minute to look at and continue to feed the intellect about what happened as we were growing up.

During adolescence, children strive to develop a sense of personal identity. Not surprisingly, children who have stumbled and lurched through the preliminary stages of human development will find success difficult at this particular stage. There are two possibilities here. Adolescents may try to recapture the magical thinking mode of youth through the abuse of drugs and alcohol. The probability of this outcome is greatly increased when such escapist behavior is routinely modeled in the home. Or this may be the stage of development where the achieving, parent-pleasing personality takes the strongest hold. For these teenagers, the need for parental approval and recognition is so high that they will be careful not to bring on the possibility of parental rejection or criticism. These teenagers will not attempt to assign motives to their parents' behavior because that would necessitate acknowledging the alcoholism, and that is too threatening.

How can these adolescents be expected to understand behavior that is taboo to discuss? Painful memories from childhood will be repressed even further. These teenagers are constantly careful to behave according to parental wishes. If they are not, the parent(s) might sense disloyalty and fly into a narcissistic rage, shrieking, "How could you do this to me?" The message is clear, the children are fine only as long as they fulfill parental expectations and deny their own. Many adult children suffer guilt feelings over unfulfilled parental expectations. Even intellectual insights into our behavior cannot relieve these feelings of guilt. The act of mourning is the only way to heal the wound of not having been loved for being just as one was. We will get to more specific information on mourning and releasing past disappointment later in this book.

The adaptations required of COAs prevent them from consciously expressing "negative" feelings such as jealousy, envy, anger, loneliness, and anxiety. The inability to recognize these feelings will follow them into adulthood, leaving only depression or some compulsion in its place. Addictive behaviors such as alcohol and drug abuse, workaholism, overeating, and overspending grow out of these neglected emotions. Precisely these so-called "negative" emotions must be recognized, felt, accepted, and mourned by the adult child. Little Miss Perfect was going to have to learn to loosen up. She was going to have to learn to feel vulnerable and stop suffering without tears. I suspected there would be some internal resistance. She had a strong investment in her position, but she left me, the adult, feeling empty, impoverished, trapped, and able to take little pleasure in my achievements. I no longer lived with an alcoholic, but my internal "parent" continued to reinforce the coping skills I had devised as a child. The time had come to bravely face the false "you are selfish" messages and place my own needs first. I began listening for other voices that might be inside of me. I heard a faint voice asking, "What about me?" I realized the abandoned Natural Child-self behind that voice was crying.

Mourning, for ACOAs, involves releasing the illusion of a happy childhood and accepting the realization of the missed attention and care. The emotional discovery, which is quite different from the intellectual discovery, and the subsequent emotional acceptance of the truth of one's childhood is not easy, but it is a necessary step in the struggle against depression. Grieving precedes freedom.

Memories, even strongly repressed ones, can be coaxed out for reexamination. Insights, dreams and fantasies can all bring clues and symbols. I have written of Karen's revelation that the arguing parts she carried within herself were actually the voices of her fighting parents. Then there is Jane, who realized at age thirty-eight that the reason she had always felt compelled to perform was because as a child she had performed in order to distract her mother from drinking. The revelations were both painful and healing for these women.

Mandy tells me of a dream she had. In the dream she is walking down the street with two small children, one holding onto each of her hands. In actuality she has no children. As they move along, the children become increasingly fussy, squirmy, and uncontrollable. Soon they are screaming, pulling back and eventually preventing all forward movement. Mandy, who is obviously the mother of these children in the dream, is unable to stop or understand their temper tantrums. She feels frustrated, thwarted, and powerless. In anger she looks down and sees that these children are her mother and father. She feels disgust at allowing them to hold her back. She raises her arms and, with a sharp shake, frees her hands from their clasp. She walks away, leaving them screaming behind her. "You can't imagine the sense of relief I felt when I woke up."

I believe Mandy's dream signaled a departure from the parenting role she had filled for her parents as a child and a clear step forward in her own recovery process. As she began to look at and work with the idea of being an ACOA, her dreams brought her symbolic solutions. Her dreams freed her.

When ACOAs begin the process of examination and recovery, they come to see and understand that childhood patterns of self-denial, alienation, and control were developed for the purpose of survival. In adulthood the patterns become unfulfilling, even destructive. The realization of wasted effort and time will bring pain and grief. Reviewing the scene of one's childhood when the curtain of denial has been drawn back is a shock. However, a true self, a Natural Child, still exists somewhere deep inside, whispering, "What about me?" This true self will begin to emerge with the process of mourning and the integration of internal voices. But first the voices must be identified and heard as separate and distinct; only then is integration possible. Hearing the voices may take some time and practice. Like Little Miss Perfect, these internal voices are parental heirs, in charge of keeping the true self isolated. But once the true self is recognized and released, that self will begin to speak and grow and develop its creativity in a drive toward expression. An unfolding imagination will begin to replace fear and emptiness.

It is only when ACOAs have reexamined the reality of their childhood from an adult perspective, found the gaps and losses, mourned and creatively tried to fill the holes, that they can turn empathetic attention toward their parent(s). True forgiveness and understanding must accept the reality of alcoholism, a disease for which the child is not, and never was, responsible. To rush this process by thinking that one "must" forgive is detrimental to the true self. Be careful here! As ACOAs we want to do what is right, what is expected, and whatever will lessen conflict. To avoid the painful step of re-feeling buried emotions and to jump directly into forgiveness is tempting. But honoring yourself and your emotions during every phase of recovery is critically important. Denial, in all of its forms, must be searched out and eliminated. Otherwise, you have only succeeded in turning your helpless victim into a martyr.

Freedom from unhealthy adaptive behaviors will begin to come when ACOAs can establish a decreased drive to please everyone, can see their parents and themselves as separate individuals, and can strive for independence without fearing parental reaction. Freedom comes when ACOAs can express ambivalent feelings, when they are no longer locked into complete loyalty. When ACOAs can fully see and accept the positive and negative aspects of themselves, they will no longer need to split off and isolate parts. They will no longer view the world as extremes, all good or all bad. As ACOAs regain access to their emotions, they increase their creative potential. The internal censors begin to lose their strength. Imagination becomes available to rejoin the intellect and the will. ACOAs move toward greater integration, balance, and vitality.

I end this section with an update on Little Miss Perfect, who does, in fact, still have a presence in my life, just not a stranglehold anymore.

Recently I was invited to meet friends for lunch at a local restaurant. After writing all morning at my desk, I stopped, bathed, dressed, and drove to the restaurant. As I stepped out of the car I realized that I had no shoes on, or with me in the car. Such an omission is not my usual style! Immediately, Little Miss Perfect sprang forth, scolding my stupidity, protecting the feelings and hurt expectations of my friends, at my expense. However, this time there was another voice, louder than hers. This voice assured me that a call to the restaurant would explain my late arrival as well as amuse my friends. This voice took pleasure in my ''being so spaced out,'' reminding me of the good, creative work I had done all morning. She convinced me that leaving my shoes at home was the healthiest thing I had done in years. For once I had let go of my preoccupation with how things looked on the outside. The soles of my bare feet were touching the ground, and I could laugh at myself without criticizing.

PART
THREE

Intimacy Overdose

$\mathcal{P}$ERHAPS THE MOST IMPORTANT THING THAT IDENTI-fying Little Miss Perfect has shown me is the untruth in a common belief shared by children of alcoholism. This is the belief that if they are just good enough and loving enough, then things will be better. This is a vague belief, especially when the "things" remain unidentified or un-mentioned. The result of such a feeling is that children take on responsibility for everyone else's feelings and behavior and wind up feeling chronically guilty.

This kind of patterning in childhood sets up the prob-ability for repetition in any intimate relationships throughout life. Adult children recognize and are drawn to repeat such unbalanced relationships. They are just trying to "get it right," to end the guilt. These patterns of interaction can become compulsive unless ACOAs get some help and develop some perspective on the dynamics of "normal" human interaction. That ACOAs are most familiar and comfortable with inconsistent attention, and that they find themselves bored with or smothered by an intimate who is capable of being emotionally available most of the time is sad.

Children of alcoholism hear many excuses for negligent behavior, excuses for irrational or angry outbursts, excuses for absences. These children bring a damaged set of expectations into adult intimacies, automatically supplying excuses instead of directly expressing needs. But being able to understand or create the reasons why people act in a particular way no longer has to excuse the behavior or erase your feelings. We deserve better treatment, and it's time we came to expect it, and stop accepting anything less.

ACOAs carry around huge reserves of guilt. They are haunted by feelings of responsibility for the drinking, for the fights, or for the parents' damaged relationship. If they are responsible, then it logically follows that they feel responsible for fixing all of those things. Because they could not fix or control everything, they learned to feel guilty because of their powerlessness.

Is it any wonder that people who take no responsibility for themselves would be attracted to those who are working overtime? Conversely, people who are overly responsible are attracted to people they can take under their wing. I think this explains why there is such a high percentage of marriages between ACOAs and alcoholics. It's a familiar and attractive pattern, at least until you stop to take a closer look. In fact, the coupling is not healthy, it is merely a repetition of the dysfunctional family relationship experienced in childhood.

ACOAs have learned to get by without adequate nurturing. They believe that they must provide all of their own support and comfort. They learn not to expect or to ask for anything from other people. ACOAs give a lot to others, but they get very little in return. Some try to fill their unmet needs by becoming care givers. They derive satisfaction and safety from giving to others because it masks their own neediness and vulnerability. ACOAs will wait and hope and keep trying harder rather than ask another person for anything. They learned long ago that asking only brought unfulfilled promises and/or punishment.

The fear of abandonment is a powerful motivator for ACOAs. Because of the terror caused by the idea of being left behind, ACOAs will take far more than 50 percent of the responsibility, guilt, and blame in any relationship. This is not intimacy, it is bribery. The fear of abandonment can also foster strong controlling behavior. Such efforts to control people or situations can easily be disguised as being helpful. Taken to the extreme, ACOAs may be compulsively drawn to people with serious problems that need to be fixed, or become involved in chaotic situations that are emotionally draining and even dangerous. Yet another manifestation of the fear of abandonment is when one partner, out of his or her panic, invests his or her emotions very deeply into the other. They desperately seize the opportunity for bonding and become deeply involved, often without much thought.

The ACOA will minimize or rationalize anything that seems to be wrong or lacking in the relationship.

What I have described here are compulsive relationship styles, addictions, if you will. This is a destructive pattern disguised as intimacy. But years of intimacy within an addictive household or with an addicted person has left ACOAs mistaking addiction for intimacy. The term being used to describe this addiction to the dysfunctional alcoholic family system is "codependency." Sharon Wegsheider-Cruse describes codependency as:

A specific condition that is characterized by preoccupation and extreme dependence (emotionally, socially, and sometimes physically), on a person or object. Eventually, this dependence on another person becomes a pathological condition that affects the codependent in all other relationships.

Any ACOAs are likely to operate as codependents as a result of their prolonged exposure to, and training under, an oppressive set of familial rules that prevented the open expression of feeling, as well as any direct discussion of personal or interpersonal problems. I believe that this early learning can be changed and that intimacy can become possible for any ACOA. This shift will require, however, a new introduction to the "V-word"—vulnerability.

Many ACOAs as well as others believe that being vulnerable always brings on negative results. This may have been your reality as a child, but the truth is that being vulnerable has an equal chance of bringing positive results and feelings. Vulnerability is the only route to true intimacy. I find, as I take the risk, that I fear the idea of vulnerability more than actually being it. My fears of being out of control, attackable, and defenseless are no longer current threats. I find that bad things can still happen whether I am guarding against them or not. I also find that I have much greater energy at my disposal since I have stopped defending myself against the threat of vulnerability. The world becomes a friendlier and more helpful place when you can allow yourself to ask for help when you need it.

This idea of asking for help is another area filled with confusion and fear for ACOAs. As children, we learned not to expect anything from anyone; it was a form of self-protection. Along with not expecting, we learned not to ask for anything, and eventually we lost even the awareness of wanting. We became numb to our desires. Lori described it to me this way:

Sometimes in the group, when they are all asking me what I need, I feel like I am being asked what I want to eat—the problem is, I've never seen food before.

You probably learned to read minds, to sense other people's moods, and to act accordingly by being helpful or by getting out of the way. You spent so much time figuring out what other people needed that you neglected yourself. You came to believe that mind reading was a valuable skill, it kept you out of trouble. But, in the absence of any other, healthier example, it got confused in your mind with love. You may expect an intimate friend to please you by reading your mind—especially since you spend so much time doing it in return. You may feel disappointed because, "He should have known that I wanted him to send me flowers for my birthday." Expecting anyone to read your mind is a set-up for disappointment. Mind reading is not a reasonable expectation in human interaction, no matter how much you may wish for it or how good you may be at doing it for others. It is a set-up for "anticipointment"—a word I made up to bridge anticipation and disappointment. It is what happens when you want and wait for something that does not materialize, either because you never asked for it, or because the expectation was out of reach. The truth is that it is harder, but much more satisfying, to learn to tell an intimate friend what you want or expect. The chances are much better that you will get what you want when you can ask for it.

INTIMACY OVERDOSE CHECKLIST

1. Do you believe that you are responsible for making _____ happy?

2. Do you believe that you are responsible for keeping _____ happy?

3. Do you take care of _____ more than you take care of yourself?

4. Are you always looking for clues about how to be more helpful?

5. Do you ever feel _____ is not grateful enough for your help?

6. Do you refuse to ask _____ for help when you need it?

7. Do you set, and then forget to honor, limits for yourself?

8. Do you make excuses for _____?

9. Do you give up doing things that you like because _____ wouldn't like them?

10. Do you think you know what's best for _____?

11. Do you finish _____'s sentences?

12. Do you imagine that _____ couldn't get along without you?

13. Do you censor yourself because you think it might make _____ feel bad?

14. Are you often giving advice to _____?

If you answered "Yes" to more than half of these questions, chances are good that you are trying to rescue another person, and that you are addicted to the process. There is a big difference between rescuing and being helpful. Rescuers never get their needs met because they cannot ask for help, cannot risk vulnerability.

Children in alcoholic homes are so focused on survival and maintaining control that they suppress their needs and desires. They grow accustomed to the lack of nurturing from the outside world and fail to learn how to nurture themselves. Or worse yet, they learn to nurture themselves in unhealthy ways, through the use of drugs, food, alcohol, spending money, or relationships. Nurture is related to vulnerability and to intimacy. It is a concept that needs reintroduction to ACOAs.

EXERCISE

Make two lists. On one list write:

I NEED TO _____.

Then fill in as many things as you can think of.

On the second list write:

I WANT TO _____.

Again, fill in as many things as you can think of.

Can you see any difference between these two lists? Does one seem more nurturing than the other? Which of the lists seems like more fun to you? Which list do you *really* want to do? Chances are that you feel more comfortable with the I NEED TO list, it is more duty bound and will not bring your "You are selfish" voices out. However, the I WANT TO list is probably more nurturing and should be worked at and incorporated into your daily life, too.

Start to look for ways that you nurture yourself and ways in which you abuse yourself. Which do you do more often? More automatically? Can you think of ways in which you would like to nurture yourself, but which you do not allow yourself? Are these sources of nurturing healthy for you?

As you identify healthy, affordable ways to nurture yourself, begin to incorporate them into your daily life. Doing this will probably bring you face-to-face with an internalized demon who shouts, "YOU ARE SELFISH." Well, look that demon right in the eye and answer, "I'M NOT SELFISH. I JUST LOVE AND TAKE CARE OF MYSELF." The more you say it, the more you will come to believe it. Making a commitment to your recovery means deciding that you are willing to take steps—no matter how unfamiliar or frightening—to help yourself. This may feel very different to you, but take a minute to think how hard you've worked to nurture, excuse, or be perfect for other people. It's time to turn all of that nurturing energy back onto yourself. YOU DESERVE IT!

Along with adopting a healthy level of selfishness, it will also be necessary to let go of the need to control other people. Being helpful and giving advice to others is a form of controlling. It's time to turn that helpful attention onto yourself. This does not mean that you must stop caring about other people, but it does mean separating yourself from other people's feelings and actions. You are not, and never were, responsible for those feelings or actions. You can care about someone without having to take care of them.

Intimacy—
The V-word
Revisited

RECENTLY, A GROUP OF WOMEN I KNOW, ONLY A FEW of whom are ACOAs, got together as a study group. One of the issues we focused on was intimacy and possible skills for creating one's ideal intimacy. I found myself ill-equipped and at a loss for words during our discussions. I had only the vaguest ideas about intimacy, and all of them were heavily clothed in fear and an automatic response to avoid vulnerability. During the first group meeting it was agreed upon that intimacy meant knowing and being known by another person, the sharing of one's essence. I found myself scribbling in the margins of my notebook:

The concept of sharing is one of my damaged areas. I don't assess mutuality in the process very well.

I began to wonder—how could I? How could any ACOAs who were trained in the denial of feelings risk the high levels of vulnerability that building an intimacy requires?

I want to back up here to explain that when I talk about intimacy I am not only referring to romantic, couple-type relationships, though much of what I have to say can apply. What I do mean by intimacy is the mutual, equal, and voluntary sharing or movement between people that enables the risking of vulnerability. Intimacy can be with the self as well as with another person, and does not necessarily imply a sexual relationship. I do believe that it is impossible for ACOAs to build an intimacy with others without first establishing a healthy intimacy with themselves.

Within an alcoholic home children receive confused and inconsistent messages of support/neglect and approval/disapproval. Most often the children struggle desperately for some semblance of order, some sense that they have some control over the environment. In the developmental process, vulnerability becomes equated with feelings of powerlessness, victimization, and being completely out of control. Is it any wonder that vulnerability is avoided in preference for rigid control and the assurance of survival? So, while COAs or ACOAs may want nothing more than to be intimate, they have learned to fear, deny, or ignore their deepest cravings.

Coupled with the fear of vulnerability for ACOAs is the threat, or reality, of abandonment, a threat that is desperately avoided by most. For ACOAs this leads to a confusion between withdrawal and rejection. In a healthy intimacy, withdrawal can be viewed as one person's movement toward his or her own self, rather than as a rejection of the other. Abandonment panic will not permit such a concept to take hold in an ACOA's mind. The threatened person will react in fear and will violate the intimacy by not allowing or understanding the other person's need for space.

In an alcoholic family, intimacies are built upon lies. Either direct lies or lies of omission. Children learn this pattern of relating in order to avoid rejection and/or disapproval. They learn to hide the parts of themselves that they think someone else will not accept. They learn not to accept themselves. Lying becomes a tool of control, a means for securing approval and acceptance. But lying brings estrangement from the self and from others, not intimacy.

You might be fuming and stamping your feet by now, insisting that you do *not* tell lies. Quite possibly you do not consciously rearrange the truth for your own benefit, but omission is a form of lying, and we have all been trained in denial, which is the ultimate omission. Try observing yourself throughout the day to see if you can catch yourself lying, or omitting the truth. I do not think that it is necessary to never lie, I just think that it is important to know when you are doing it, and why.

The following is a list of words and phrases that the study group came up with to describe the concept of intimacy. How many of these qualities do you honestly have with yourself? How many do you share with others? Is there room for improvement in your intimacies?

QUALITIES OF INTIMACY

Unquestioned trust

Open, direct, and honest communication

Belonging

Warmth

Gentleness

Love

Listening

Allowing nurture

No obligation

No guilt

Healthy, mutual conflict resolution

Emotional expression is encouraged

Self-acceptance

Acceptance of others

Privacy

Respect for independence

Respect for limits

Safety

Honesty

As I said to begin with, the whole concept of intimacy was a bit of a mystery to me. As the group generated this list, I grew increasingly agitated by a growing awareness of my own intimacy deprivation and the fear that popped up as I entertained the potential. There was a part of me that wanted to shout, "Oh, it would never work anyway," and protect myself from feelings of vulnerability—the dreaded "V-word"!

For yourself, reread this list slowly and try being aware of the feelings and mental images that come up for you. Try making your own list of qualities found in intimacy. Try to imagine, and then describe for yourself, an ideal intimacy. (Remember that this does not necessarily mean a romantic attachment.) Examine what already exists in your life that approaches what you imagine as an ideal intimacy. This is a good exercise for getting acquainted with what may be a very unfamiliar area of human interaction for you.

I believe that the process of recovery for ACOAs requires the construction of a healthy intimacy with the self, with the Natural Child as well as the Adapted Child. This involves reacquainting ourselves with all aspects, both good and bad, and accepting them. Intimacy with others will be flawed without the prior establishment of a healthy intimacy with the self.

So, how does one go about building an intimacy with the self? How does one build intimacy with another person? What are the required skills? What are the tools? Here is a list that our study group came up with. Feel free to add your own ideas or to delete any that you do not find useful on this list.

INTIMACY SKILLS

Honesty, telling the truth, being able/willing to hear the truth

Direct expression

Listening clearly without judgment

Setting limits for yourself and honoring them

Letting go of control over others

Self-acceptance

Self-observation

Defining problems

Articulating concerns

Negotiation and compromise

Creating a safe space

Seeking support for personal growth and change

Willingness

As I look over this list, I cannot escape noticing that each and every one of these intimacy skills would threaten the typical survival strategies learned by children and adult children of alcoholism. This is a point that cannot be passed over lightly, it needs a closer examination.

Honesty, telling the truth, hearing the truth. Direct expression.

By looking back at your alcoholic family, it is probably getting clear that what you were told was not always the truth, at least not the truth you are beginning to recognize in recovery. You may have been told that everything was all right and not to worry, while your senses, your intuition, and every nerve ending in your body was sending you a very different impression. You learned, willingly or unwillingly, the family code of denial and silence. In order to survive the chaos and escape punishment, you stopped hearing the truth and you stopped telling the truth. The differences between the truth and lies became blurred. Direct honesty could not be tolerated or sustained in your home, so you learned to survive without it. The drinking caused problems, but everyone was forbidden to talk about them; everyone conspired in a lie. Trust broke down in the family and honest communication was lost as a result.

Intimacy requires honesty rather than obedience, and a willingness to express that honesty openly and directly. The lies need to be recognized and then the denial and the lying must stop before intimacy can begin to develop.

Listening clearly without judgment.

Listening may be something that you do quite well, and you may also be able to suspend judgment. Children from alcoholic homes usually take in a great deal of painful and confusing information without any chance to process it. They learn how to listen but not to respond, not to ask questions, and certainly never to contradict. This passive form of response does not threaten the alcoholic parent, so COAs remain safe while appearing attentive and respectful.

The problem here for adults is that in order to build healthy intimacy, people must listen to and try truly to *hear* what other people are saying. Listening alone is not enough. Intimacy requires some honest response on the part of the listener; it requires the listener to be in touch with his or her feelings and the willingness to risk sharing them. Intimacy requires opening up to the experience of listening and responding to another, not just steeling oneself for the ordeal.

Setting limits for yourself and honoring them. Letting go of control over others.

The inconsistent parenting behavior characteristically experienced in an alcoholic home is not a good model for parental limit-setting. Children do not get reliable responses from parents and so become distrustful or fearful of the chaos. As a result, children may self-impose strict limits on themselves in an effort to secure some sense of control over the environment and their emotions. This strict, controlling limit-setting is not the same thing that is required in an intimacy. In fact, it is quite the opposite.

Children are powerless to set limits, and without appropriate parental models the skills will go unlearned. By setting limits I mean deciding what is acceptable and what is unacceptable behavior in other people. Defining what you will and will not tolerate in other people and letting them know that. The next step is to honor those limits. After setting them, it is your job to let people know if they have violated one. This is not the same thing as trying to control others' behavior. You are only

85

concerned with your response. You are not responsible for other people's reaction. You can assert yourself without having to change them. This way, each person has equal importance, rights, and responsibility—a prerequisite for intimacy.

When I met Little Miss Perfect, I began to see that I had not learned to set proper limits for myself. I had allowed her to set the standard, in response to critical parental messages, and in adulthood she was strangling me. She drove me to compulsive perfectionism as a substitute for love. She controlled others by being better or more prepared than they. She kept others at a distance in order to protect her fragile self-esteem. She was a survivor but she left me feeling anxious, self-critical, and lonely. She may have been in control, but she was incapable of intimacy.

Self-acceptance—Self-observation.

Self-observation is the window into personal change. Unless we can see ourselves, we cannot change ourselves. Wanting to change may sound contradictory to self-acceptance, but I don't think it is. Observing ourselves, deciding what we would like to change or improve about ourselves, while always accepting ourselves just the way we are at the moment is important. Acceptance can be fluid—we can accept ourselves just as we are while we are becoming what we desire.

Parent(s) within an alcoholic home are typically critical, if not outright condemning. Children learn to turn this criticism inward onto themselves. As adults, these children can learn to release the old, negative messages and to replace them with accepting words and realistic images.

Defining problems—Articulating concerns.

As a child, you probably learned pretty quickly that talking about problems in your house either got very little attention from your parents or else it got you into trouble. So, you learned to ignore or to avoid seeing or talking about problems. You began to wonder if you were crazy because you were the only person who noticed that things were not quite right. You either stayed quiet in your confusion or you stopped seeing the problems altogether.

If you were punished or silenced for speaking out, it will be extra threatening for you to reclaim your perceptions and the ability to articulate them to others. But these skills are necessary for any sort of intimacy. Without them, you will be making someone else completely responsible for everything in the relationship.

Conflict is a much avoided area for most people, but especially for anyone whose childhood was surrounded with it. What ACOAs do not learn is that conflict can be healthy and dynamic. It does not always have to be horrible or life-threatening as it might have seemed. Conflict can be exciting; it can even be a spark between two people, an intelligent challenge, or a way to get to know someone better. Conflict no longer needs to be avoided in order to survive; in fact, it needs to be courted in order to achieve intimacy.

Negotiation and Compromise.

Do you remember ever hearing or seeing your parents negotiate? Do you remember them reaching suitable compromises together? Do you remember thinking, "Now that's the way I want to act when I grow up"? Chances are good you don't remember these things. It is much more likely that you heard fighting, name-calling, and slamming doors as one person stormed off. You might have had to listen to physical abuse, or suffer it yourself. You probably vowed never to act like them and gave up thinking that compromise was a possible option.

Now, as an adult, you're not so sure how to deal with people or situations that are not turning out just like you expected. You may feel powerless to do anything about a bad situation, just like when you were younger. Maybe you just withdraw emotionally or leave the situation completely rather than try to talk to someone and reach an agreement.

There is another twist here, too. Maybe your home life was so tumultuous and unsettled that you grew accustomed to that level of chaos. Maybe you feel bored when everything is going along smoothly and you don't feel like you're on a roller coaster gone berserk. Maybe you need conflict and chaos to make you feel connected. Maybe you don't want to compromise because then you might risk feeling bored and disinterested.

The establishment of intimacy with another person will involve some sharing and some giving and taking on both people's part. You may have to take it completely on faith to begin with, but after some practice, hopefully you will begin to see the possibilities and feel good about them.

Creating a Safe Space. Seeking Support for Personal Growth/Change.

Risking intimacy and trying to practice new skills can be a frightening process for anyone, but especially so for ACOAs. I think that it is important to acknowledge the scariness and to admit it to yourself so that it will not keep popping up for you to stumble over. Admitting that anything scares you may be a very new experience, but it is an important step in recovery.

Imagine that a little child has just told you that she is afraid of the thing that the two of you are preparing to do together. What would you do? You might spend some time explaining to the child that there is no danger, assuring her that you will be careful and that you will protect her. The time and attention spent will help ease the child's fear and make the experience more enjoyable. The child will trust you because you listened and promised not to let her get too scared.

As you begin the process of self-observation, mourning, and creative change, there will be much that comes up to scare you. Don't deny that fear, and don't try to force it into the closet. It won't go away that way anymore. The Natural Child still left inside of you needs more care and attention than that. Imagine having with yourself the same soothing conversation that you had with the child. This process honors the small child we carry inside and helps to create a safe space for trying new things.

The rapidly growing numbers of support groups for COAs and ACOAs attest to the increasing numbers of people who struggle with the same pain and confusion

89

that you and I do. These groups encourage members to share, to trust and to be vulnerable. A support group experience of this type might be an excellent beginning for intimacy skill-building.

Willingness.

The point may be self-evident, but without a willingness to recover or change, ACOAs will get nowhere. I want to urge you over and over again to be gentle with yourself. Change does not happen overnight, and you have to honor your own pace. Self-examination can be painful, and there may be times when you will want to back off or stop the process completely. Give yourself permission to move at your own speed. Be as willing to be patient with yourself as you are wanting to get healthy.

Through no fault of your own, you've probably never had the chance to experience a healthy intimacy. Now you can have the opportunity to start exploring and learning. It is my belief that ACOAs can learn new and healthier patterns of human interaction and intimacy, but this learning will require courage and a willingness to trust and take risks.

Once ACOAs begin taking responsibility for themselves, they can then choose to share themselves with someone else in a truly intimate relationship. They will begin forming relationships out of choice rather than falling into dependency or overresponsibility. They will develop relationships and friendships that are mutually beneficial and enhancing.

PART
FOUR

Roadblocks, and the Road Map to Recovery

CHILDREN WHO ARE SURROUNDED BY CHAOS AND CONfusion tend to split their worlds into absolute opposites, into black and white, good and bad. Thinking in rigid terms is more comforting for these children than entertaining complexity. This compartmentalizing process goes on throughout life, leaving ACOAs feeling unconnected, unsatisfied, and quite possibly sick. The process of recovery attempts to reconnect adult children with their experiences, desires and creative potential, but there are roadblocks along the way.

ROADBLOCKS

Intellectual Understanding

One such roadblock to the process of recovery is the belief that an intellectual understanding of a problem will somehow miraculously erase it. This approach is too passive and too private. Experiential learning is necessary for any ACOAs whose early learning process was interfered with, but you have to *do* something. This book is full of experiential learning exercises that can be done privately, with a friend, or in a group situation. Some exercises involve taking risks and trying out new behaviors. Remaining in your comfort zone of familiarity will not bring about healing changes.

As you begin the process of recovery, be on the lookout for your tendency to react to newness in an old, "Yes . . . but" way. Be careful not to let fear or laziness prevent you from trying new things, getting healthy, and having a good time.

Anger

Another roadblock is ACOAs' unwillingness to let go of anger, to let their parent(s) off the hook for past mistakes. Some ACOAs prefer to remain in the position of righteous victim/martyr rather than move on to the difficult task of recovery and forgiveness. I know this because I spent many years feeling powerful and invulnerable while wrapped in a cloak of anger and spite. It wasn't until I noticed that the cloak was also choking me that I began looking for ways to get out of it.

Anger is an emotion found hiding in most families, but especially in an alcoholic one. There is the anger of disappointment and broken promises, the anger of abuse and neglect. Unexpressed, discounted and denied, but anger all the same. Because we grew up in an atmosphere where no one dealt appropriately with anger, we never learned how to handle the feeling. We may even feel frightened by the mere potential for anger, our own or others'. Common fears include the following:

"If I let my anger out, I will explode, or destroy everything in my path. I will be completely out of control—I might even kill someone."

Feelings of fear further encourage ACOAs to deny any feelings of anger. They may be successful in completely obscuring the emotion. But anger remains, shoved down and ignored until the threat of an explosion is real.

There are other ACOAs who are consumed by their anger. I was like this for many years. I spent most of my time in what I now call "Outrage Mode." I was critical and dissatisfied, and I regularly went on verbal tirades in an attempt to vent my frustrations. I was mad at the world, traffic lights, traffic, the weather, anything that I was powerless to control. But when it came time to honestly share feelings of disappointment or anger with another person, I shied away or lied. In this way I protected my righteous anger without having to confront the real situation. It took years of work to see that my outbursts were disguises for other negative emotions that I couldn't or wouldn't name, or that made me feel too vulnerable to admit. Outrage was my smoke screen against vulnerability.

Anger is a very real and valid emotion that our culture and our families teach us to ignore or keep under control. We are not taught how to creatively express any negative emotions, and in the process other emotions become confused with anger.

Taking some time to focus on what you have learned about anger is helpful. Take some time and some paper, or your journal, and try to honestly think about and answer these questions for yourself. When you were angry as a child, what happened to you? Were you punished? Were you shamed? Were you ignored? Were you listened to? Were you told not to feel that way? When your mother/ father got angry at you, what did you feel like? What did you feel like when they got angry at each other? Were you scared? Did you feel guilty? Did you ever not understand why he or she had gotten mad? Did you try to talk back, to defend yourself? What happened then?

Now, take another piece of paper and answer some questions about your anger today. What internal messages, ideas, fears keep you from expressing or even feeling anger? What is your worst fear concerning anger? What is the worst thing that could happen if you got angry? What is the best thing that could happen? Do you see any differences between your answers from childhood and your answers today? Are there things you would like to change about how you feel, express, or respond to anger? Please remember, it's never too late to refashion things you told yourself or learned as a child. You just have to be willing to try.

If you are trying to focus on anger and nothing will come to you but the idea, "I never get angry," then try looking at your dominant emotion, the emotion that you feel most often. I mean, if you are always afraid, or sad, or depressed, look and see whether that emotion is really masking buried feelings of anger.

Depression is described as anger which is directed back onto the self rather than outwardly toward an appropriate target. Depression is commonly suffered by both alcoholics and their families. Is there any wonder, since the healthy resolution of feelings is so retarded by the family system? Avoiding feelings of depression will require learning to feel, experience, and express a wide range of emotions, including anger.

Denial/Body Awareness

The constant and automatic messages of denial which children incorporate as they grow, will eventually cut them off from any normal body awareness. They will not equate a stomach ache with an emotion or a behavior. The body may be screaming for attention, but ACOAs in denial will not listen. Just as the alcoholic does not listen, but has learned to quiet the screaming with another drink.

As a small child, in an attempt to attract love and attention, you may have complained of countless aches and pains. If this attention-getting maneuver served its purpose and you did in fact get some attention, there is a good chance that as an adult you are still exhibiting aches and pains that could be considered hypochondria. The sad fact is, when we repeatedly "tell" the body that it is sick, it will eventually respond to our messages and *become* ill.

We all got messages about illness and health from various sources as we were growing up. These messages will stay with us forever unless we consciously do something to change them. The following exercises can generate some useful information about the particular messages that you learned or told yourself about illness and health. The following examples are some of the early ideas that I concocted about sickness. Try completing this same chart for yourself.

"I LEARNED TO BE SICK FROM":

Person/Experience	Explanation	Message
My father	He ate antacids like they were candy	"I have a nervous stomach."
The school nurse	She would listen to me and take my temperature when I complained of feeling bad.	"I'll take care of you, now don't you worry."
The TV	I was hooked on Dr. Kildare and Ben Casey.	"If I'm sick, people will care for me and love me."

Did anything pop up on your list that surprised you? Were you able to make any new connections about your state of health as it relates to your mental state, or what you have been taught about sickness?

Another method for learning to pay attention to the messages from your body is to try to track the origin of one of your most common physical ailments.

—What does it feel like? (Dull? Sharp? Relentless? Burning? Tight?)

—When does it occur? (When you're going to visit your family? On the job? In the middle of the night? Whenever John calls to ask you out on a date?)

—What does this ailment prevent you from doing? (Going out? Performing duties? Sleeping? Enjoying life?)

—What does this ailment encourage you to do? (Take aspirin? Stay home? Feel sorry for yourself? Feel lonely? Have a drink? Ignore it?)

—What reward does this ailment bring? (Feeling like a victim? Acting like a martyr? Avoiding unpleasant or difficult situations?)

—What deeper need is being signaled? (Need for attention? Need for love? Asking for things? Getting your needs met?)

—Is there a more direct way to get this need met? (Learning to ask other people for things or assistance?)

Another exercise involves imagining that you are having a conversation with a part of your body or with a physical symptom. This requires imagination and the suspension of critical judgment. You can talk out loud or use your journal for this exercise. It is important to get relaxed first. If this is hard for you to do, please read carefully the section on breathing. Once you are feeling relaxed, start talking to this body part or symptom as though you were trying to get to know some new person.

—When were you born?

—Where were you born?

—What do you do for a living?

—What is good in your life?

—What is bad in your life?

—What gives your life meaning?

—How did you get here?

Please add any questions that can help you get whatever information you need. Next, imagine that the pain or the body part can and does answer your questions. *Do not censor anything that you hear your body telling you.*

"I was born when you turned away from your mother and went to your room without telling her how mad you really felt. I am a pain in your stomach that wants you to talk to her, to get the anger out. I will feel much better then."

"I am a swollen foot that acts up every time you have an opportunity to make a change, and then get too scared and lose the chance. I want to take steps to get better, but as long as you won't permit those steps to be taken, I am going to swell up and cause you pain."

"I am twenty extra pounds around your body. I'm here to protect you from feeling hurt again. No emotional pain can get through this armor of fat."

"I am a sore throat that shows up whenever you are silencing yourself. Whenever you refuse to take care of yourself, to speak up for yourself, I will show up in your throat."

There are many different answers that you might hear from your body. Listen for the metaphors in your physical symptoms. I think you will be surprised by these exercises if you will allow yourself to be completely honest and open with yourself.

Take a Deep Breath

For the most part, breathing happens without any need for conscious direction by the breather. Breathing is not something we *do*, it is something we allow. Breathing is the only system in the body that can be controlled either voluntarily or involuntarily. But left alone, the body will keep breathing. What is important to recognize is that we do not always allow breathing to happen naturally. We do things to restrict our breath and deprive ourselves of the energy that oxygen provides. It is time to pay some attention to how we block our breath.

All emotional states produce physical changes in the body. Some emotions will increase tension in the body and add to the restriction of breath. Conversely, regular breathing can return the body to a balanced state where tension is reduced.

FEAR: The first reaction to fear is to gasp for air. The body becomes rigid, and the breathing gets shallow. It feels as if the air has gotten thinner, or that there simply isn't enough of it to breathe. When the danger has passed, the body can relax again, and normal breathing is resumed. But observe yourself if you tell someone about the frightening incident. Just recalling the details can cause the body to recreate all the tension, the sweaty palms, and the shortness of breath. The same phenomenon is true when anticipating frightening situations; before the fear is even present, the body goes through its physiological preparation. Keep in mind how much of the time you may be anticipating scary situations, then take a look at how you are breathing.

GRIEF: The inability to breathe freely is also a common reaction to grief. You may feel like someone is standing on your chest. It's also like your chest muscles get hard in order to protect the heart from further trauma. But the result is a shortness of breath, which in turn will cut off the painful feeling. Deep crying, or at least sighing, is necessary for working through the experience and attendant feelings. Releasing grief will take the weight off the chest and allow normal breathing to resume.

Repressed emotions such as fear, grief, and anger are common among COAs and ACOAs. It is possible to consciously learn to use the breath for expressing these emotions openly and honestly. Conscious breathing will also activate the parasympathetic nervous system and produce relaxation. ACOAs have a lot to learn about breathing. We have learned to suppress emotions, and we have desperately tried to protect our hearts. It's a wonder we don't all have blue faces and chronic hiccups. It is time to take a look-listen to your breath.

Note to Smokers: That smoking reduces oxygen intake and inhibits normal breathing is a well-accepted fact. But the habit of smoking develops in a way so as to perpetuate itself. When faced with a difficult situation or emotion, smokers automatically reach for and light a cigarette. Just when they need more air, they cut off the supply. Smokers come to mistake the first inhalation of smoke as a calming substitute for fresh air and true relaxation. Slowing down and taking a few deliberate deep breaths is a far healthier way to release distress and anxiety.

The in-and-out flow of breath reminds us at all times that we are alive. But we get used to it and ignore it. Instead, we spend time thinking about the past or the future, and we miss the moment that we are in right now. As you become more conscious of your breathing, you will be more a part of your present, and you will feel more relaxed.

Nearly all relaxation techniques employ the use of conscious breathing. Stress management, yoga, meditation, biofeedback, and even natural childbirth are all popular examples in which deep breathing is used to produce relaxation.

Begin to pay attention to your breath. Take time during the day to observe your posture, the tension in your body, and the depth of your breathing. I suspect you will find yourself tensed up, taking shallow breaths. When you find yourself like this, take a minute to take in a few slow, deep breaths. Inhale through your nose and push the air out either through your nose or mouth on the exhalation. Making noise as you do this will increase your awareness of the breath and the relaxation that accompanies it.

EXERCISE: TAKING A FULL BREATH.

This exercise will show you, perhaps for the first time, what taking a complete breath really feels like. Try it sitting, standing or lying down, whichever is most comfortable for you.

Exhale deeply—Contract the stomach muscles.

Inhale slowly as you fill the abdomen with air and expand it.

Continue inhaling as you fill the chest with air and expand it.

Continue inhaling and raise your shoulders up toward your ears.

Hold the breath for a few seconds (only as long as it is comfortable).

Exhale in the reverse pattern, slowly. Relax your shoulders and chest, contract your stomach muscles.

Repeat.

Roadblocks, and the Road Map to Recovery

I've mentioned several roadblocks on the road to recovery. I know these because I've been stopped by them on my journey. Take some time to see if you can identify any of your own specific barriers. Write them down, acknowledge them, know that they are there and that they need to be moved out of the way. This, in itself, is a healing step forward on the road to recovery.

RECOVERY

Just as we learned how to be unhealthy within our alcoholic homes, we can reverse that learning. The process of recovery is just that—the reverse of involuntary, automatic and often, quite destructive thought and behavior patterns. Recovery is a deliberate turning around of some of what we learned or designed earlier in our lives.

Breaking out of familiar patterns of thought and behavior will require letting go of strict logic and control and then stepping into the unfamiliar realm of possibility. Children know how to do this instinctively, but COAs quickly learn that such an indulgence threatens their security.

Children play for the sake of whimsy and fun, not because they expect results from the game. So, enjoy your process of self-discovery and try not to judge your process or expect it to turn out in any one particular way. Try to adopt the attitude of attention and absorption that you had the first time you listened to a fairy tale or a story being read out loud. You were not directing or anticipating the outcome, but you were completely wrapped up in the excitement and magic of the story.

Could you go back and become a great friend and guide to yourself as a child? Can you even find that child anymore? Try to think of a time, when you were a child, when you would have been very receptive to the arrival of a sympathetic stranger. Picture that child standing in front of you now, needing your help and support. Picture that child, because he or she still exists and is there asking for you. It is still possible to help that child feel more powerful, more secure and resilient, even if you cannot change his or her experience of childhood. This is the process (of recognizing/identifying the split-off and neglected parts of yourself) that precedes re-integration.

As children, we learned to dull our perceptions (Mom and Dad fight all the time and I feel scared) and to replace them with conceptions (That's just the way adults are, now don't worry). Now is the time to reverse that process, to begin to reconnect our thoughts, feelings and experiences, and to fully live our lives.

By allowing information from our senses to once again inform us, we begin to conceive of our new possibilities. We begin to believe in what we see. We begin to trust our perceptions, and we begin to trust ourselves. As we become sensitive observers, we develop new delight and wonder that freshen our perceptions and allow the all-too-familiar shroud of depression and helplessness to lift. Learning from the patterns of our lives is movement in the direction of a life with increased potential.

Recovery is a choice.

Recovery is a movement toward the optimum.

Roadblocks, and the Road Map to Recovery

Recovery is a lifestyle you design to reach your highest potential.

Recovery is a process—there is no end point, but health and happiness are possible once the process begins.

Recovery requires discipline.

Recovery brings an integration of body, mind, and spirit.

Recovery is a loving acceptance of yourself.

Recovery is freedom.

Recovery is very much like an exercise program—you must be actively involved before positive results can begin to appear.

The process of recovery for each individual person will be unique, just as different people's experiences with the disease of alcoholism are both similar and diverse. Individuals bring different interests and levels of willingness to explore the process of recovery. Respect yourself, go at your own pace, and honor whatever seems of most interest and meaning to you along the way. There is no right or wrong way to go once you choose the route of recovery.

Healing is based on connections—connections between body and mind, thought and action, and intuition and the outside world.

Western culture teaches us to separate the mind from the body, while the fact remains that the mind and body

107

are the same. The body is commonly ignored in favor of the rational mind, thereby cutting us off from a wealth of information that comes through and is stored in the physical body. The body has the same ability as the mind for remembering and storing experience and information. I believe that in recovery it is time to challenge the tyranny of the dominant perception: Thought. To reconnect with feelings that we rejected with our rational minds, we *must* begin to acknowledge all the receptors available to us. It is useful to begin trusting and using the body, the subconscious mind, and any other nonrational signals and allies.

In the first chapter of this book, I shared my experience with guided imagery. That initial session allowed an insight to become accessible to my conscious mind. It was my first clue about what lay ahead for me in the process of recovery. Admittedly, at that time, fear caused me to turn away from the challenge. But the new awareness never left me.

I have talked of naming the various aspects of the self so that they can become recognizable, and so that they can communicate directly and clearly with the conscious mind. These techniques may seem like games, and perhaps they are, but what's so bad about games? Games require playfulness, and playfulness comes from the Natural Child hidden deep within each of us. Games might be just the answer for reacquainting ourselves with this child and winning his or her trust back after all the years of neglect.

When the body, mind, and spirit are connected, a person will have plenty of energy and vitality. When

108

energy is blocked, a person becomes sick. Healing is affected when blocked energy is released. Emotions can be expressed freely, and a positive mental attitude is maintained. We all have the power to heal ourselves. Healing is an act of love, a journey deep within oneself. Healing is the reuniting of body, mind, and spirit. Healing is the gradual process of becoming more self-aware. Illness is not necessarily anyone's fault, but healing is everyone's responsibility. There are choices to be made all along the way and questions to be asked.

Who am I and where am I going?

How am I feeling and why?

What needs to be done to change my current situation?

What needs to be done to change my feelings?

What steps am I willing to take to change?

Children from alcoholic homes learn a confusing message about responsibility. When they see a parent shifting all responsibility to something outside ("I had a hard day at work today") children internalize the responsibility (I know it is all my fault). This imbalance is unhealthy. Both sides suffer from dis-ease. The process of recovery for the alcoholic and for ACOAs involves developing healthier levels of self-responsibility and love.

Self-Responsibility

Recognizing signals from your body (headaches, tense shoulders, loss of sleep, constipation, sore throat).

Discovering and honoring your own needs.

Making choices without feeling guilty or responsible for others' feelings.

Creating the life you want rather than continuing to react to what is happening in your family.

Being self-assertive.

Taking care of your health, your physical body.

Expressing emotions honestly and clearly.

Creating and cultivating intimacy with others.

Doing work that is meaningful to you.

Love

Trusting yourself.

Learning from dis-ease.

Responding to problems rather than sinking into victimization and self-pity.

Affirming yourself.

Loving yourself, including your weakness.

Realizing your connection with all things.

A quick look at these two lists could easily bring the word "impossible" to the lips of ACOAs. The changes and the huge levels of trust required to make them may seem overwhelming and far too scary. But, if you can view these lists as a series of suggestions, rather than assigned and mandatory tasks that must be done immediately, perhaps the list will become less frightening.

Take a deep breath and remember to keep breathing, especially when you feel anxious or scared.

Managing Your Stress Before It Manages You

Sometimes I think that Little Miss Perfect's life force is fueled by stress. The busier and more anxious I get, the more likely it is that she will gain complete control, smother my Natural Child, and drive me unmercifully from task to task without ever stopping to appreciate that things are, in fact, getting done.

My first introduction to the concept of stress happened in 1978 when I attended a workshop on stress management. I was asked to "relax" and try to find areas in my body where I held tension. Relaxing was a bit of a mystery for me, but a quick survey of the tension in my body led me to the conclusion that tension must be what held my body together. It was everywhere, and it seemed I might be jelly without it.

Throughout the workshop we learned various exercises for reducing stress and tension. By the end of two days I had a completely new awareness of myself, and the ability to relax, as well as a pretty good assurance that I wouldn't turn into jelly.

A large part of the problem for adult children is that we arrived into adulthood completely unskilled at managing stress. As children we were powerless over stress; we learned to ignore it or to run away. As adults we still ignore or deny our stress. But the stress itself has not gone away.

You might have thought that your parents caused your discomfort, while actually, the distress came more from your responses to their behavior than from anything they did or did not do. The cause of your distress is internal, not external. But this does not mean that it is all your fault; it just means that you can do something about it, if you are willing to take responsibility. It is possible to re-interpret stressful events into positive opportunities.

One of the by-products of stress is a feeling of being overwhelmed. The best way I have learned to diffuse the stress is to do one thing at a time, and try not to worry about anything beyond that one thing or that time. Little Miss Perfect has often had a hard time adjusting, but this way my attention stays focused in the present, things get done and my anxiety is lessened.

How many times has all the time and energy that you spent worrying about something made the situation any easier? Is it necessary to worry whenever you are presented with a new or difficult situation? Or is this just a conditioned response to feeling out of control? Worry is stress and it needs to be lessened. Once again, one step at a time seems to be a good approach.

Whenever I begin a new project, I notice that I reawaken my worry-bug.

What if I'm not good enough?

What if no one agrees with me?

What if I look stupid?

What if I can't do it?

What if my ideas are all wrong?

What if . . . . . ?

What if . . . . . ?

What if . . . . . ?

When I let the what-ifs go on for too long, I can get myself into a state of high anxiety that paralyzes me altogether. This is when I need to stand back, take a few deep breaths, and focus my attention on one small aspect. I usually even have to set up a specific program for myself to follow until the stress is lessened.

Example: Today I will complete this one part of the project without expecting anything more of myself.

or

Today I will take time out for some deep breathing whenever I notice myself feeling anxious.

or

Today I will not allow telephone calls to interrupt my concentration.

or

> Today I will work for four hours and then
> reward myself by going swimming.

These guidelines help me to slow down and keep stress away.

As ACOAs become more familiar with themselves through the practice of self-observation, they will also get acquainted with their own stress pattern—what starts, what maintains or perpetuates their stress and distress. Once again, awareness is the first step toward change.

The following disciplines and exercise are all popular forms of stress management:

Yoga

The science of yoga assumes that the body and the mind are part of one continuum of existence. The interaction between the body and the mind is of central concern. It is believed that as the mind and the body are brought into balance and health, the individual will be able to perceive his or her true nature. This perception, in turn, will allow life to be lived more spontaneously and freely.

Yoga attempts to reach the mind, where health begins. Mental choices can strongly affect the health of the body, just like diet and exercise can. Yoga permits the natural state of total health and integration within each of us to manifest into reality.

Yoga changes the way we think about our bodies. We become aware of our strengths and weaknesses, where we are tight and what moves freely and easily. This increased awareness leads to healthier choices about diet and exercise.

The physiological changes caused by the practice of yoga include reduced blood pressure, lowered pulse rate, elimination of stress, and subjective feelings of increased well-being. Yoga restores a state of balance in the body.

Mental health is another goal of yoga. Through learning to watch the movements of the body and the breath, the yoga student is brought into the present moment. Focusing and refocusing on the moment is a necessary step toward letting go of old patterns of rigid and neurotic behavior. Another goal of yoga is to eliminate old patterns that inhibit the full expression of creativity and the enjoyment of life.

Yoga can transform the typically unhealthy mental attitudes of ACOAs. Rather than sublimation and elimination, which are fostered through the practice of denial, yoga produces transformation. Yoga is an integrative force, allowing the students to become more fully what they already are. Yoga accepts inner nature, it is life affirming. It is a process and a goal—just like recovery.

Meditation

Meditation is a conscious activity used for quieting the mind by stopping the flow of images and thoughts. It is a technique for cleansing the mind of all fears and releasing creativity and energy.

Powers of concentration must be developed before

meditation can be practiced. Relaxing and attending to the in and out flow of breath is a good way to start. Next the attention is focused on a single image. A burning candle can be a good image to concentrate on, or you can create a mental image of your own. As other thoughts arise in the brain, concentrate on bringing your attention back to your image. This kind of attention focusing will take time to learn. It is a good idea to practice, if only for several minutes every day. By setting aside a specific time each day for meditation, you will begin to establish a habit in your mind. Be sure to set a pace for yourself that you can meet. This way the new habit can grow and develop. As your powers of concentration develop, lengthen the time you spend meditating.

Since the mind and the body are basically functionally identical, the calming of one can produce calm for the other. Can you remember a time when your mind felt very confused? What did you do? I have found that if I engage in some ordering-type behavior with my body (cleaning out a closet or going to an exercise class) my mind calms down and becomes more orderly as a result. This is the idea behind the practice of meditation.

The mind has tremendous power to contribute toward psychological and physiological well-being. The practice of meditation can take a variety of forms, but certain aspects are common.

POSTURE: The spine is kept straight; the weight of the body is balanced, not tense. Many believe that the posture of the body reflects and influences the inner posture of the mind.

Roadblocks, and the Road Map to Recovery

IMMOBILITY: Just as there is a time and a benefit in movement, there is also a time and a value in stillness. Refraining from movement can have important strengthening effects on self-confidence. The capacity to suppress any movement can free the mind.

DISCIPLINE: Discipline involves organizing one's day around activities that have meaning and value. These activities will contribute to a stronger sense of self-worth. The commitment to meditation is a commitment to the self.

FOCUS: Meditation involves focusing the mind on a single object. This practice supports relaxation and reduces stress. It can lessen anxiety merely by providing an object for the attention.

ATTENTION: All meditation involves passive attention: the mind is open to whatever enters it, here and now, letting go of controlled awareness. When passive attention is combined with relaxation, there can be a natural lessening of previously learned anxieties and fears. This is psychological healing at its best. The body is deeply relaxed, feeling no fear, and various unconscious and semiconscious memories, images, and thoughts will rise to awareness. When this happens, there can be a reduction in the negative emotional charge that these memories hold. Meditation can be an invaluable tool for self-examination and grieving.

The time we can take each day for meditation is important. This quiet time is used for contacting one's inner power as well as one's Higher Power.

At deeper levels of meditation, there's a state in which the meditator forgets the self and surrenders personal patterns of malfunction. Letting go of the mind in this way can promote the release of paranoia, which makes us think that we are isolated individuals, struggling in a hostile and indifferent environment.

Meditation relaxes and heals the body, makes the mind efficient, creative, and intuitive, and results in more balanced, integrated, and harmonious personalities. What ACOA could pass this up?

Helping a Robot to Play

Even if we are sitting perfectly still, we are still in motion. The heart is pumping, blood is flowing, and the lungs are expanded and contracted. Because of this movement everything in the body is changing from moment to moment. Movement can change one's inner world as well as one's outer world. But change can be blocked if the natural movement of the body is blocked. While it is true that the body is constantly in motion, it is the quality of that motion that will affect the quality of your life.

Clearly, there has been a dramatic change in the exercising life-style in America. In fact, we might have gone a little overboard. Streets are clogged before and after work with runners and bicyclists. Tennis courts are booked days in advance, and exercise studios crop up daily. The primary emphasis seems to be on "fitness," often marketed as "weight reduction," but rarely promoted just for the sheer fun of it. Whether or not you enjoy exercising, the fact is that exercise makes you feel good—not just physically, but emotionally and spiritually as well. Exercise reduces stress while also aiding in weight reduction and muscle toning.

My personal interest in exercise is focused on the potential for fun as well as for psychological growth and change. One problem I see with most exercise programs is that they are not individualized. Individual differences and needs are not respected, and the attendant emotional responses are ignored. What pleasing/obedient ACOA isn't going to try to do the 500 leg lifts suggested by the instructor, and try to do them all the very first day? Consequently, many exercise programs are discontinued and feelings of guilt and self-loathing get reinforced.

My first introduction to aerobics happened before I had fully identified and named Little Miss Perfect. But it was certainly she who was donning leotards and dragging my aching body to a two-hour workout every morning at seven. At first I was pleased by the apparent self-discipline, but after a few months I began to notice the signs and symptoms of an addiction. As I strapped more and more weights to my wrists and ankles and began doing repetitions double-time, I pushed myself to the outer limits of my endurance.

One day a friend suggested that we visit another studio and I agreed, secretly hoping that I would be challenged in some new way. The challenge turned out quite differently. The music was light and playful, not the driving beat I was used to, and the movements were free-form and mostly individual. I was suddenly freed from the robotic motions that I had drilled into myself and found myself skipping and prancing around the room on my own impulse. It was as if a five-year-old child had suddenly been set free inside an adult's body. It was great fun and my Natural Child was delighted.

Finding an exercise program which will be fun as well as helpful is important. Time spent exercising is time spent with the self, so don't make that time punishing. You might even try asking your body what sort of exercise it would like to do. You'll be surprised at how the body responds when you begin paying some attention to it.

SELF: "What would you like to do today?"

BODY: "Oh, I'm so glad you asked! I'd really like to go for a walk."

SELF: "A walk? But what about aerobics class?"

BODY: "I'd rather go for a walk. I want to be outside and I want it to be quiet. Some days I just can't stand to hear all of that music that they play at the exercise studio. It puts my nerves on edge, I'd rather go for a walk today."

SELF: "But the workout is so much better there."

BODY: "We've done the workout together three times this week. Can't we take the day off and do something that I want to do? It's still exercising, you know."

SELF: "Oh, all right. I guess I'd sort of like to go for a walk today too."

A good exercise for starting the process of getting acquainted with your body involves standing in front of a full-length mirror, without clothes on, at least once a day. Be careful here! The purpose of this exercise is *not*
120

to critically check yourself out for millions of flaws and imperfections, though that may well be your first inclination. The purpose *is* to become familiar with your body and, if need be, to alter your self-image into a healthier one. This is an especially difficult and important exercise for women, because women have been socialized, more than men, to hate their bodies and to judge themselves against an unrealistic standard. It is important, while performing this daily body reading, to make sure that you view both sides of your body. We want to deal with your whole self these days, not just those parts that are attractive and easy to see.

While you are spending this time with yourself in the mirror, it might be a good idea to practice some affirmations. As you stand there, repeat out loud to yourself:

I love myself and my body.

I am becoming the person that I wish to be.

I take good care of myself and my body.

My body, mind, and spirit are becoming healthy and whole.

I listen to my body and respond with respect to what I hear.

I do not push myself mercilessly. I allow my body to move at its own pace.

Physical exercise is a perfect complement to the process of recovery. As ACOAs open their hearts to vulnerability, they also protect them with the physiological benefits of exercise. People who take an active interest in keeping the body healthy usually display other healthy characteristics. Their stress is lower, their self-confidence is greater, and they have healthier eating habits.

Beware, though, as I found for myself—exercising can become a compulsion in the same way that eating, drinking or smoking can. For ACOAs there is a particularly high probability for compulsive behavior. A strong need for control can easily lead to a rigidly imposed self-discipline of exercise. While the physical result may be a desirable new body, excessive exercising can become another addiction, a form of emotional armoring if you will. Be aware of your motivation and of what you are trying to achieve through exercise. If your goal is "hardness," *beware!*—this is control in disguise! It is possible to be mentally and physically strong while still maintaining flexibility, openness, and emotional vulnerability. Remember to keep *fun* as one of your goals. Lastly, don't set yourself up to feel inadequate. Start slowly and build yourself up. If you push too hard and try to be perfect from the start, you will probably not enjoy yourself, you might hurt yourself, you might discontinue the activity, and then, worst of all, you will probably wind up feeling guilty. None of that is the purpose of exercise. Some guidelines to keep in mind are:

—Make fitness a part of your life—not just a crash program.

Roadblocks, and the Road Map to Recovery

—If it's not fun, don't do it.

—If it hurts—Stop.

—Don't be a robot—let your body be playful with movement. Be spontaneous with your body. Try to remember how you moved as a child.

—Reward yourself for every effort at exercise, no matter how long you did it. (Like if you walked for fifteen minutes, give yourself credit rather than a hard time for not going for forty-five minutes.)

PART
FIVE

Does This
Playpen Come
In Extra Large?

I HAVE USED, IN THE EARLIER PART OF THIS BOOK, examples of dreams, insights, guided imagery, and journal entries to illustrate the avenues through which new information, not always of the rational variety, can be received. Information alone, however, is insufficient for creative personal change. Insight and understanding must be followed by action. In this section I want to explore how anyone, but especially ACOAs, can use such tools for personal growth and expression. The goal is to recapture the playfulness lost in childhood, and to bring it into balance with the logic and intellect that are the steadying anchors for most ACOAs. This balance, which allows for the expression of all one's capabilities, is the basis for mental health.

The process for rediscovering lost aspects of the self requires the searcher to have the desire and the belief that cause him or her to expect success. This trust is not readily forthcoming for rigidly trained ACOAs. Furthermore, the process involves taking risks, doing the unexpected, and just waiting to see what happens. I will not minimize the terror that such a process can uncover. However difficult and frightening, I have found that the effort is both rewarding and fun.

This book is written primarily from my personal experience, my studying, and my intuition. If some of the exercises in this section do not work for you, skip them or make up your own variations. If something you read sparks either your memory or your creativity, stop and take some time to give yourself the chance to have the experience. Be as playful as you can with yourself as you do these exercises. There is no right and wrong here, only an opportunity! The answers come from what the work brings up in *you*. They do not come from the outside.

I believe that the support of a group experience can be both encouraging and safe, but I also know that the idea of sharing information, not to mention feelings, with strangers can be utterly terrifying for anyone, especially ACOAs. I have, therefore, illustrated exercises here that can be used privately, with a therapist, or within a group setting. Please use this book in the way that best serves your need.

Because children and adult children of alcoholism suffer alone, they feel great isolation and confusion. When you grow up this way, believing that no one else ever feels the same as you, it is hard to trust. Therefore, sharing such feelings in a supportive group setting, or with a close friend or relative, can be therapeutic. Only through the process of being listened to and truly heard by another person can you begin to validate your feelings and experiences and begin to feel "normal." You might want to work with a therapist, with a close friend/fellow ACOA, or within a supportive group setting. And you might choose to do a lot of your self-observation and mourning work alone. Just remember that a great deal of support is available if you can ask for it.

Try answering the following questions in your journal, or with a friend.

1. How many children were in your family of origin?

2. Which one of your parents drank?

3. What was said about drinking in your home when you were a child?

4. Complete the sentence—"I was the one in the family who always _____."

5. If there had been a banner over the front door of your childhood home, what would have been written on it?

6. If there had been a banner over your room, what would have been written on it?

7. What, if anything, seemed the most forbidden to you as a child?

8. What is your earliest memory?

9. How would you describe your childhood? (short phrase or word)

10. What gave your life meaning when you were a child?

11. Do you remember having an active fantasy life as a child?

12. What were your favorite stories as a child?

13. Did you ever have an imaginary friend or an alter ego as a child?

14. What did you think you would be when you grew up?

15. What did you say you would *never* be?

16. What were the happiest times in your childhood?

17. Who was a special person to you as a child? (teacher, grandparent, brother, sister, etc.)

18. How would you describe yourself to someone who didn't know you?

19. How do you think that your parents have influenced your adult life?

20. What is your present relationship with your alcoholic parent(s)?

21. Do you think that your past interferes with your present? With your future?

22. Name three things that you most enjoy doing. Do you do these things regularly?

23. What gives your life meaning these days?

24. Complete the sentence—"I am because I _____."

25. What do you imagine/hope to happen in your future?

JOURNAL KEEPING

A journal-keeping teacher, Kay Hagan, describes the journal as, "The door that is a mirror that is the self." The journal spans all time frames. It can be the past, present, and future at the same time. The journal does not demand the writer to make logical, linear sense. It is a place for play and creation. The journal can become a personal design board—a place to chart progress, goals, and dreams. It serves as an anchor during confusing periods of personal change—a place to find the balance between pain and joy, anguish and optimism. THERE IS NO JUDGE WITHIN THE PAGES OF YOUR JOURNAL.

I have always been a journal-keeper, with greater or lesser frequency. By looking back at old journals and diaries I have discovered experiences and aspects of myself as a younger person that I had forgotten. And I have found patterns in my behavior of which I was unaware. I found Little Miss Perfect and my "I am afraid" messages inside the pages of my journal. The same day that I recognized that fearful messages preceded my dreams, I also heard a faint voice, urging me onward. I named this voice Freeme. Freeme has been a great help throughout my work in recovery. She constantly reminds me not to get caught behind my fear. She can take risks, and I am glad to let her.

Within the safety of the journal I began looking for still other hidden aspects of myself, parts of my Natural Child that had gone into hiding when I was a little girl. The most important person I have found is Mimi, my true child-self, my Natural Child. Mimi is Little Miss Perfect's shadow side, a playful, free-spirited, and often quite "naughty" little girl. I have learned to work with these different aspects of myself to counteract the censoring voices of my Adapted Child. I have developed playful strategies, like engineering a mud fight between Little Miss Perfect and Mimi, to keep myself from getting stuck in old, rigid patterns of obedience and repression. Within the safe pages of my journal I allow and encourage the adapted and freer aspects of myself to discuss, or fight out, the alternatives.

Mimi's enthusiasm is taking hold. The promise of play is tempting. "Why not?" Little Miss Perfect whispers, testing the words, feeling the shivers run faster up her spine. "Why the hell not?" she shrieks in open rebellion. Both girls are floating on the wave of their own mischief, carried beyond the rough water of their own scrutiny.

Walking toward the river, Mimi released Little Miss Perfect's hand, reached down and picked up a handful of mud, rolling it into a ball as Little Miss Perfect squirmed uncomfortably beside her. "Don't be such a priss!" shouted Mimi as she landed the mudball into Little Miss Perfect's chest. A satisfying splatty sound preceded the surprised laughter that escaped from Little Miss Perfect.

Reaching up, Little Miss Perfect smears the mud around, pulling more up to her face and hair. She is tap dancing with delight in the squishiness.

This exercise helps prevent the automatic, adapted side from immediately taking control, while also attending to previously ignored parts of the self. The process is balancing and shows respect for the true child-self, the Natural Child.

I believe ACOAs get thrown out of balance by being asked to be rational long before they are developmentally ready. The creative, intuitive and inventive parts of a child are lost as that child meets and incorporates the strict rules surrounding family alcoholism. The culture colludes by reinforcing rationality, and the adult is left feeling vaguely out of kilter. The journal is a safe place to explore the illogical side of yourself and to confront scary or confusing feelings.

I found a word to describe a voice, a feeling in my head. And once I had this word I could touch myself in a different way. The word was SPITE: To hurt oneself to get another's attention. But it only hurt me—no one else ever saw.

We are at the hospital. Each lonely room along the dim corridor holds its own sad story. A once-familiar gentleman, with eyes now sunken, skin turned yellow. A man slapped down by his own hand, which nurses have now lashed to the side of his bed. This man used to hold me in his arms.

A journal is an invaluable companion on the journey of self-exploration. However, if your privacy was ever violated during your childhood, finding the sense of protection that you will need for honest and consistent journal work may be difficult. Can you think of some way to confront the feeling of invasion that you suffered when your privacy was not respected? Can you set up a place to write in your journal that will not be violated now? Can you let go of your fear of invasion?

If you can make it a safe experience for yourself, the journal can become, possibly, the first place where you can truly develop a strong sense of intimacy and trust. To finally find a safe place to talk about and explore all that has been previously forbidden is a healing experience. The journal will provide you with the total attention and acceptance that were typically unavailable within your alcoholic household.

When I talk to myself about what stands in my way, I imagine myself inside a box. I am a tiny person inside a slippery-sided box. Sort of like a Jack-in-the-Box. My parents have put me in here and I keep expecting them to come and get me out. "Forget it!" I hear somewhere. So today, instead of waiting, I'll imagine myself growing, taller and wider, until I won't fit inside the box. When I am bigger I can step out with ease. In this new, bigger body, I will stroll past all of the clouded mirrors in my parents' house. I will no longer stop and try to catch

134

my reflection in any of them. I will escape and I will be free.

The act of writing involves more parts of the brain than does just thinking. Therefore, it can often be quite a surprise to go back and read what you have written.

If you are still not convinced that there are parts of yourself that work to sabotage your efforts, take a minute to listen for the voice that calls you from the kitchen, demanding that the dishes be washed before you spend time with yourself and the journal. Do you recognize this voice? Do you welcome it? You might also listen for the critical censor who is on your shoulder, whispering questions and breathing doubts into every word you write. You can learn from these voices if you can resist the temptation to judge and dismiss them. Remember, it was the rejection and suppression of these parts of yourself that sent them underground and made them angry in the first place. Acceptance and attention will bring about the desired balancing and integration of the self. Playfulness comes in when ACOAs can gain enough detachment to name the different aspects and negotiate with them, much like Mimi's mud fight. Be careful not to criticize any aspects of yourself, no matter how surprising or disappointing they may appear to you. Ellen describes her process this way: "Writing in a journal gives measure to my dread, goals to my obsessions, and faces to my demons. I don't have to fight anymore. Everything is labeled. I can decide now. The decision will be truly mine."

Writing is not the only descriptive medium that can be used in a journal. Many people record pictures, collages, dreams, and short fragments of conversation, or insights and impressions that they find enlightening. Since the hope is that a journal can help to unlock blocked potential and creativity, the more ACOAs can play within the pages of a journal the better.

A few years ago, when I started keeping a "working journal" as opposed to a "recording journal" (Dear Diary, today we went to Disneyland), I got stuck, or rather Little Miss Perfect got stuck, in the belief that there was one "right way" to keep a journal. She was much more willing to follow assignments than to allow me free expression on the blank pages. I negotiated a truce by following journal exercises until Little Miss Perfect calmed down. By acknowledging her need for structure, and not expecting myself to throw off years of internal limitations, I was able to find a successful way to use the journal.

Remember, there is always a voice inside of us that will resist knowing about anything new, who will staunchly uphold the family rules. Watch for where resistance is strongest; there is something to be learned there. Try to appreciate and embrace the resistance; this will lessen the fear.

The following suggestions are possible journal exercises to follow if you find that you have nothing to say when confronted by a blank sheet of paper.

1. —Make a list in your journal of all of the roles that you have played in your life. (Child, student, worker, spouse, parent, etc.)

   —Can you think of names for these different roles that illustrate how you played them? (Little Miss

Perfect, Sally Stopwatch, Goody Two Shoes, Mr. Hardhead, etc.)

—How do you feel about these roles as you put them down on paper and name them? Are they still serving a purpose in your life? Do you need to revise their job descriptions?

2. —Make a list of your negative selves. (Jealous Person, Revenge Seeker, Praise Withholder, Procrastinator, Late Thank-You Note Writer, Gossip, Loner, Perfectionist)

—Be careful here.

—Most ACOAs are so filled with self-loathing that the entire journal volume could be filled with this list of negative selves. The point here is to identify, *not to condemn.*

3. —Ask each of these negative selves to tell you, in writing, why they do what they do?

—You may start by asking them what they need. Why are they angry? What do they get from doing what they do? Why do they work against you?

—Notice how you talk to these negative selves. Do you nag? plead? whine? bargain? insist? How do they talk back to you?

4. —Listen for the critical voice who criticizes you. Is there a chorus, or just one voice? How does it/they justify the criticism? What calls it into action? What precedes the criticism? Can you talk back to this

voice? If you did, what would your posture be? What would you have to say?

5. —What do you criticize in others? Is it in you, too?

—This can be a place to find the "shadows," those dark sides of the self that are hidden.

6. —Listen to how you talk to yourself as you go through the day. What is the intention of your internal dialogue? Do you accuse yourself? Do you taunt yourself? Do you punish yourself or do you nurture yourself?

7. —Observe how you react when someone praises you or pays you a compliment. What do your internal voices answer?

—Observe how you react when someone criticizes you. What do your internal voices answer? Which voices are the loudest, those that react to the praise or the criticism?

—Notice whether you feel that these voices have your best interest at heart. Can you negotiate with them? Can you enlist their support? Are they "on your side"?

8. —Observe your inner "resistors," or anyone who slips out to sabotage when you are having a good time.

—Learn what sets them off. What are they afraid of, and what do they need to feel less frightened? Can you negotiate with them?

9. —Identify something that you expect from life, something that you hold onto fiercely and which life has not yet provided for you.

   —Watch how this expectation distracts your attention from other areas of your life. How could you become more patient, more trusting? How could you quell your longing? Is this expectation a reasonable one to hold onto, or is it only hurting you?

10. —Observe when and where you tend to feel sorry for yourself. Do you try to enlist others to feel sorry for you too?

    —Observe what causes you to fall back into the position of being a victim.

11. —Write your own personal myth.

    —Write a myth for your family.

    —Remember, a myth is something that never was, but is always happening.

12. —Make a collage of your family. What are the colors and shapes that you are attracted to using? How do you represent different family members?

    —Write about how it felt to do this exercise after you have completed doing it.

13. —Take an old family photograph, look at it carefully.

    —Tell a story about each of the people that you see in the picture. Make up things if you want to and just let your imagination run wild, see what comes out.

139

—Assign new personalities to the characters if you wish.

14. —Make a doll for each different member of your family.

—Make a doll for yourself.

What sort of decorations will you put onto these dolls? What colors? Are the dolls smiling? Do they move? Are they soft and snuggly, or stiff and brittle?

—Write about how it felt to make these dolls after you have finished.

15. —Make up a dance about yourself.

—Make up a dance about your family.

Why do you or different family members move in the ways that they do?

16. —Keep a dream journal in which you record your daytime and nighttime dreams. (There will be more about a dream journal later.)

17. —Invite your child-self to take a walk with you. What does this child notice? What are his or her impulses? Was s/he willing or reluctant to come with you? Were you willing or reluctant to ask? Does your child-self walk beside you, in front of you, or behind you? Does your child-self seem to trust you?

18. —Make note of any creative ideas, fantasies or thoughts that come to you during the day. Don't worry if they are incomplete or make no sense. Just write them down so that you will have a record of

your inspiration and/or flashes from your intuitive mind.

—Don't force ideas to come and don't criticize yourself if they do not come easily at first.

I hope these suggested exercises will help you get started with working in your journal. Also, they may inspire your imagination to come up with your own ideas for exercises. The journal is a useful companion for any of the exercises and techniques mentioned in this book. It can be where you record the exercises as you do them, or where you chronicle your feelings, impressions, and new learnings. It is your personal record of your struggle and journey toward greater fulfillment and recovery. The point is to have fun while also learning about yourself and working to heal deep pain, so try not to set journal work before yourself as a "task." Otherwise the journal will take on the unpleasant aspects of a chore, and the benefits will be lost.

The following examples demonstrate some of the creative techniques used by ACOAs who are working hard to regain spontaneity and to get out from under the influence of family alcoholism.

Examples of Journal Entries

"I wrote my own myth. First of all I got stuck in the middle of it and I couldn't finish it. But the part that came out was that my father emerged, not as a villain, but as someone who had been a warrior in another land and who had been wounded. Then he had been introduced to something that would heal him, but the price was so great. The price was forgetting who he was, and in his forgetting he would become violent."

I particularly liked this example because it incorporates the fairy-tale-like qualities of providing symbolic reasoning while also giving Emma, the adult, some clues for "why" her father acted in forgetful or violent ways. Almost as though she were providing a reason for herself to be able to forgive him.

"I feel like I'm really on track now after almost thirty years of trying to figure it out. I've done serious work ... years of sitting in front of the typewriter in intense introspection, wondering why I am so screwed up. For example, when I was 22 to 26, I would spend the whole day at the typewriter doing self-analysis."

"When I was a child, I remember my sister coming in while the whole family was supposed to be decorating the family Christmas tree. It was a yearly event, and it usually ended in an argument about something. Well, this particular year my sister marched in and announced in her eleven-year-old wisdom, 'Our family Christmas tree isn't decorated in ornaments, it is decorated in arguments!' I have never been able to forget the statement, and every year I get depressed when I think about having my own tree and decorating it. Last year I decided that I wanted to break the spell of my childhood memories. I had a small party, bought lots of art supplies and asked my friends to help me make Christmas tree ornaments. I now have a lovely box full of handsome ornaments that have special and healing memories for me. I am starting my own rituals for the holidays, and I no longer have to tote around all the unhappy memories and the arguments."

"When I was nine years old, I read about Amelia Earhart. I became fascinated and read everything I could find about

Does This Playpen Come In Extra Large?

her. My parents really helped me to pursue her, and at age nine, I basically fell in love with her. Her vision of wanting to fly is how I avoided what was happening in my home. I was her, Amelia, and I intended to fly. I still dream about flying. I'm sure it has to do with escape. One of the things that I did as a child was paint one whole wall of my room with airplanes across it. There was a series of windows, huge ones across one wall. What I looked out on was trees and blue sky. I painted the airplanes all around the windows, so that when I rolled over and lay in the bed, that is what I saw. That wall was a total fantasy for me. All I had to do was roll over and lay in the bed and I could just take off, and that's just what I did."

"I started in the center with an emotion I 'knew' the least about because it was never mentioned in my home. But it was also the emotion I was coming to realize that I felt most often. I just never had had a name for it, so I acted angry instead. I wrote it down and just started to free associate, to build a molecule of it. What came out was sort of a surprise to me. This is my feeling cluster."

(Items for feeling clusters)

143

"I learned a lot about myself and about what I had been taught about fear by doing this exercise."

More Feeling Clusters

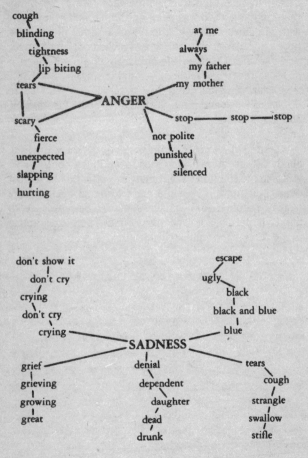

DREAMS

Lately I have been having dreams in which my parents have been poisoned. I am trying to get them some help, but no one will help me, instead they accuse me of having given them the poison. It is a very frustrating and guilt-producing dream, but it's also an intuitive window into which I need to focus my attention. I attribute the dream to my fears of repercussion over breaking the alcoholic family rules: Don't Talk, Don't Trust, Don't Feel.

Dreams are messages from the psyche that reveal it to us. Dreams offer glimpses into one's rich inner world; they try to balance what is out of balance in one's conscious life, and they offer guidance for living. Dreams can give us knowledge of our hidden talents and unused creative energies, as well as information about the negative, neglected, or repressed parts of ourselves. Dreams can point to where changes need to happen in our lives, warn us of dangers, and confirm our beliefs. Dreams magnify and intensify feelings in order to bring them to our attention. Dreams are trustworthy because they come from the wisdom of the inner self, from the intuition. Dreams can enrich our lives by opening up new possibilities. Dreams bring messages from many dimensions. Dreams speak in images and pictures, using symbols that are both universal and uniquely personal. To understand your dreams you must give them the attention and respect they deserve. You must establish a dialogue with your dreams until their messages become clear.

I have already provided several examples of dreams

145

that brought specific insights to the dreamer. Now I would like to offer some hints for how to improve your access to your dreams.

The first rule of thumb, especially for eager ACOAs, is to *be patient!* If dreams are not already easily accessible, it may take some time and practice before they can be clearly remembered in the morning. Don't expect or push yourself to be perfect at this right away. Try to remember that "being perfect" really means going at your own pace, while working hard.

Another word of caution for rational-bound ACOAs is that accessing dreams will require trust in yourself and a willingness to let go of your stranglehold on logic.

Try not to get overly concerned with analyzing your dreams at the beginning. It is better to get into the habit of remembering and recording your dreams. Analysis can come later when you begin to see patterns that emerge from your subconscious mind.

Keeping a Dream Journal:

1. Give yourself a suggestion before going to bed at night. "I will remember at least one of my dreams when I wake up in the morning."

2. Keep a notebook, a pen, and a flashlight (or better yet, a flashlight-pen) beside the bed so you can write down the dream immediately upon waking. *Do not* try to convince yourself that you will remember the dream again once you have gotten up. It doesn't work that way. Dreams are like mercury, they slip

away very quickly without the proper handling. The sooner you write the dream down, the more detail you will be able to recall. Another idea would be to keep a tape recorder beside the bed and record the dream while it is still fresh in your mind. You can then transcribe the dream into your journal.

3. Write your dream down in first person, present tense, as though you were still in it. This will help to trigger your memory. Write everything down as fast as you can. Dreams disappear from our memories very quickly.

4. Write down every detail you can remember. Do not analyze, justify, or edit anything as you record your dreams.

5. Note everything, even if you can't tie it to anything specific. Example: A purple vase, but you can't remember where, when, or why it was in the dream, or any other object, person, or sound that doesn't seem to fit logically into the dream.

6. Later, when you are really awake and want to work with the dream, you may want to add the current details of your life at the time that this dream occurred. For instance, what was taking up your conscious time and energy at the time you had this dream? What were you wishing for, and anything else that feels important to add.

7. Dream researchers claim that everyone who appears in a dream is a representation, or an aspect of the

dreamer. Therefore, you may want to explore what is being represented about you by those other characters. Do you recognize any of these characters as your internal voices?

Be careful not to get swept up into analyzing each and every aspect of your dreams. The point here is to increase the information flow from your intuition to your intellect, *not* self-analysis.

The ability to remember dreams is more an attitude than a specific technique. What is needed is a true desire for self-knowledge, trust in the healing potential of dreams, receptivity, prompt documentation, and an appreciation for the images in dreams.

Personally, I have found that when I make a conscientious effort to remember my dreams and do not succumb to the temptation of laziness that makes me turn over and fall back to sleep before recording, I actually begin to remember more detail with greater frequency. Also, whenever I am working very hard in my conscious life on a particular issue, my dreams work overtime as well.

Dreams reveal, in symbols, how you face important conflicts in your life. Often dreams will dramatize these conflicts over and over again until you begin to pay attention. Dreams can even give you a variety of creative solutions to your problems.

I have a recurrent anxiety dream about missing airplanes. There are several variations to this dream. In some I am waiting for a ride to the airport, getting increasingly anxious and irritated as the time runs out. In others I am already at the airport, but I cannot find the correct gate. There is no one around who can give me directions. And in yet another version I am headed toward the right gate, but as I get closer and closer I am losing the ability to walk. I get stiffer and stiffer until I cannot walk at all. The end result of each version of this dream is literally a crippling sense of powerlessness and frustration.

As I started working with these dreams, I discovered that I either could not find anyone to ask, or else I asked people for help who could not give it to me. The point finally got through to me one night when I watched myself in the familiar dream. I am walking, then crawling, and eventually I am dragging myself across the floor to get to the plane. There are people all around me, but I am stuck and refusing to admit my helplessness and ask for assistance.

A few nights later I had another version of this dream. This time I am waiting for a friend to come by and pick me up. He is going to take me to the airport. My friend is late, and when I call to remind him he sounds calm and tells me to relax. I am filled with rage because my urgency is being ignored, and I am going to miss my flight. I am pacing back and forth, feeling hopeless and angry, when another idea occurs to me. I suddenly see that I could call the airport and change my reservations to a later time. The idea brings a flooding relaxation with it. I no longer feel anxious, angry, or out of control. It was a very useful insight and broke the pattern of those anxiety dreams. This dream helped me open a door onto new responses to old problems.

AFFIRMATIONS AND CREATIVE VISUALIZATION

I am a loved and loving person.

I can make mistakes and still be a good person.

I am patient with myself and with the process of recovery.

Holistic thought states that life is a circle and that each individual has responsibility for creating and maintaining the harmonious whole. The body, the mind, and the spirit are not separated and can therefore work together, reducing antagonistic elements and resolving tensions. Through such balancing, humans can gain greater self-worth and self-love and begin to reconnect with others.

For such holistic resolution to take place for anyone, but most especially for ACOAs, it requires new learning. Resolution, as opposed to conflict, requires seeing and speaking to the goodness in ourselves and others. This will help in breaking the conditioning of criticism that we all know. Filling the mind with positive images can happen only when negative images have been released rather than repressed. These new, noncritical messages are called affirmations.

We were taught, inside our alcoholic homes, to look outside of ourselves and to react to what was happening in "appropriate" ways. Our focus on the present got skewed by dwelling on the past or looking fearfully into the future. We were trained to judge, analyze, predict, and control. To just "live in the moment" always felt too threatening. Resolution requires that we begin to look inward and live more completely in the present. As we learn to do this, even trivial moments will begin to shine. Every moment can become extraordinary when we pause to truly look at it and experience it.

Using affirmations enables a person to change negative thought patterns into positive ones. Affirmation is the antidote to criticism. We begin to see each moment as a chance to begin anew. This attitude can bring you a long way from the attitude of blaming in which you remain a victim. It takes a courageous choice to set aside fears and work toward greater wholeness, change, and risk.

Ideally, healthy, well-balanced individuals use both hemispheres of their brain with equal ease. Recent research into brain function has shown that each hemisphere has clear and distinct abilities. In reality, our culture favors the logical, linear abilities of the left brain. These qualities are trained in schools and rewarded in the workplace. If the ideal is the integration of both hemispheres, it is important to know what each side does.

LEFT BRAIN	RIGHT BRAIN
Logic	Recognition
Reason	Rhythm
Mathematics	Visual Imagery
Writing	Synthesis
Language	Dreams
Analysis	Symbols
	Emotions

151

I have argued throughout this book that ACOAs, because of their stunted period of childhood, get forced into rigid, left brain function at the expense of the right brain. Fear, worry, an unwillingness to try new things, being judgmental or overly controlling are all functions of the left brain and will not lead to creative resolution. However, the expression of fun or whimsy is more conducive to a shifting to right brain function. The sad part is that our society rewards adherence to the logical side of our brains, and as adults we remain out of balance and unable to access the childish, playful, and healing potential within ourselves. Balancing is merely a matter of acquiring new information and training oneself to use it. The negative messages learned during childhood need to be replaced with more positive, healthier ones. The subconscious mind does not discriminate or judge, it just obeys. The brain has remarkable abilities to reeducate itself.

Affirmations and creative visualization are easily learned self-improvement techniques that engage aspects of each brain hemisphere. When used together, integration and self-enhancement are the result. Each technique works to raise self-esteem and thereby aids the process of self-exploration and personal change.

An affirmation is a deliberately chosen positive thought placed before one's subconscious in order to produce a desired result. It is like a creative "what if . . . ?" that suspects the best instead of the worst. "What if I could have or be anything I desired or dreamed of?"

The process of using affirmations involves repeating a positive phrase, then watching and recording any internal resistance that arises from the subconscious, then continuing to repeat the positive thought. The exercise works to change old, negative messages into current, positive messages. The use of writing, reading and language engage the familiar left brain, while the right brain plays a part in creating the affirmation. It is not always necessary to sit and write out the affirmations, you can just repeat them to yourself as you go through your day. But, to get started, it might be a good idea to use the suggestions I am providing.

As I mentioned before, the journey toward personal change and improvement requires a *desire* to change, the *trust* and the *belief* that change is possible, and the *expectation of success*. Such attributes are not readily forthcoming in ACOAs, who are unaccustomed to personal power or the fulfillment of expectations. Affirmations can help to develop these attitudes. John is a clear example of someone in need of an affirmation.

> *I would say now, that despite the fact that I do well at a lot of things, there is still a feeling of self-doubt, that I don't quite belong. So, I'm a fake in a sense. No matter how well I do, and even when I think I am doing well, I also feel like it's not really true, I can't do that. It was never good enough.*

So, how do you create an affirmation? An affirmation is a simple sentence, stated in the present tense, which expresses something that you wish was reality as though it already was. Or, an affirmation can be a positive assurance that you provide as support for yourself during times of personal stress and change. To create an affirmation, think of the qualities you wish to affirm about yourself, then state those qualities as simply as you can.

I, ___(name)___, deserve to recapture my playfulness.

I, _____, get and deserve to get approval and love from my world.

I, _____, have the courage to face pain so that I can heal from within.

I, _____, am a strong, centered, and creative person.

I, _____, am surrounded with loving, supportive energy.

I, _____, am doing the very best that I know how at all times and do not need to criticize myself.

One way to use affirmations is through the process of writing them down. First, create your affirmation. Then, write it down ten to twenty times on a piece of paper.

I, _____, am a creative person.

I, _____, am a creative person.

I, _____, am a creative person.

I, _____, am a creative person.

I, _____, am a creative person.

Does This Playpen Come In Extra Large?

As you write this phrase over and over, repeating the message to your brain, your subconscious mind will begin to react, sending up conflicting, even combative messages. As you hear your own rebuttals, jot them down to the side or on the back of your piece of paper. These countermessages provide excellent clues for what stands in your way. They are the reasons, subconsciously, why you keep yourself from having, or being all that you desire.

No way!

You're not an artist.

So what?

I'm stupid to be doing this.

They'll never recognize me anyway.

I'd be more creative if my parents had loved me more.

I hate them for ignoring me.

The barriers thrown up here suggest that this ACOA is still being limited by the tendency to blame rather than to change. However, the information generated by the subconscious resistance can suggest other affirmations such as:

I, _____, am not in competition with my parents.

I, _____, deserve to live my own life, a life that I have chosen and created for myself.

I, _____, am a channel for creative power.

I, _____, love myself and deserve to be happy.

It is good for me to risk being myself. I do not always need others' approval. I trust myself.

I try to use affirmations specifically because creative energy has to flow into us through our beliefs, attitudes, emotions, and habits. The wounds suffered as we grew up have constricted our beliefs and habits to such an extent that they slow, distort, or even completely block the flow. The affirmations can help in releasing useless beliefs by replacing them with positive, supportive ones.

The repetition and the attention to the interfering messages from the subconscious, Adapted Child's mind, produce the desired awareness and changes in self-esteem and a sense of internal power and potential.

Obviously, a journal can be an excellent place to record these exercises. The counteracting messages will provide clear windows into the internal censors, the saboteurs and the Adapted Child.

Creative visualization is a technique that employs consciously chosen visual images to produce changes in the body and behavior. It is the reverse process of imagining negative outcomes. Creative visualization encourages us to see and expect success. To begin the process, the imagination conjures a desired image, thought, or way of being. Next, the visualizer engages his or her senses and entire body with the image. Noticing scents, sights, tastes, textures, and sounds, indulging fully in the desired image. Through the use of such strongly felt imagery you can begin replacing unhealthy brain programs and expectations with healthier ones.

Dreams and insights can provide clues for the process of visualizing change. Try to remember that your thoughts and beliefs are what create your present-day reality. You are responsible for creating the life that you desire and dream of.

Research clearly shows that visual images, in which a person is deeply and emotionally involved, can influence the body and behavior. A strong image leads to behavior consistent with the mind's-eye image. In the same way that an ACOA, like Nancy, imagined applying asphalt to her emotions, the process can be reversed. Earlier a healing vision was explained by Karen, who imagined the divorce of her internalized, quarreling parents.

Doctors are beginning to realize the healing power of visualization along with the possibility that chronic pain may arise from self-inflicted emotional punishment inside the patient. Any ACOAs who fail or refuse to release their feelings of responsibility and guilt for parental drinking and/or marital discord will continue to punish themselves and fail to achieve personal liberation or satisfaction in adult life.

If you are feeling a little skeptical about the power of imagery and the effects on the body and behavior, just take a minute, close your eyes, get relaxed and think about the Christmas holidays. Pay attention to any changes in your body. Are you still relaxed? What do you see, smell, taste, touch, and hear? Has your mood changed? Different people will be stronger in certain senses. Try to find the sense that brings you the most information. When you think of rain, do you smell, taste, hear, feel, or see it? What about horses, pancakes, babies, birds, spring?

An example of creative visualization is Mandy's dream in which she saw her parents as children, tugging on her arms. The children were acting like brats and preventing Mandy's forward movement. In this case, Mandy's subconscious mind sent up information that she could use toward personal change. The image of herself as parent provided her with the power of choice, an unfamiliar feeling for her. Symbolically, she realized how the childish, self-indulgent behavior of her child-parents was impairing her ability to get ahead with her own life. She worked with the image, combined with affirmations, to help her get over the extreme guilt she felt for letting go of her caretaking role, to release herself from the feeling of unnatural responsibility she had toward her parents. Her self-image was enhanced by the ability to release her sense of duty and guilt.

Dreams, intuitions, messages from internal censors and revelations all provide information that the conscious self does not possess. It is important to trust your intuition and to do what feels right for you without looking to others for approval, especially not to those specific "others" who have withheld it for all these years. For anyone coached in rationality and discouraged in creativity, this trust will have to be deliberately constructed. Affirmations are a good place to start.

I, _____, open myself up and welcome information from my subconscious mind.

I, _____, trust myself and my inner guides.

I, _____, am proud of who I am.

I, _____, deserve to state my needs simply and clearly to other people.

I, _____, deserve to have my needs met.

I am lovable.

Nobody is perfect. I don't need to try to be perfect.

Everything that goes wrong is not my fault.

If bad things happen, it does not mean that I am a bad person.

I, _____, deserve to be loved.

I, _____, can learn to trust others. I give myself plenty of time to learn this.

I, _____, no longer need to think I will fall apart if someone leaves me or rejects me.

I, _____, can clearly communicate my feelings, ideas, and wishes.

I, _____, no longer need to be in strict control of myself and others.

I, _____, can give up control and still trust in my survival.

I, _____, have a right to all of my feelings.

I, _____, do not need to constantly apologize for myself.

The right brain, or metaphoric mind, is inventive. It lacks the knowledge that something is impossible. It is hopeful and optimistic. ACOAs typically need increased access to such reservoirs of optimism. The right brain can provide an excellent antidote to the highly critical and judgmental internal censors of the left brain. My vision of recovery for myself and any ACOA comes when invention, playfulness, and a return to fantasy can replace rigid conformity, automatic responses, and guilt. I believe that ACOAs are then well on their way out from under the influence of family alcoholism.

The following are some exercises that you might want to try. Feel free to create your own variations.

Make a list of the names of people throughout your entire life who you feel have mistreated, hurt, or harmed you—people toward whom you feel anger and resentment. Next, write down, beside their name, what it was that they did to you. (I find it helpful to use a different small piece of paper for each person.)

Close your eyes and relax. Take each sheet of paper, one at a time, and visualize that person standing in front of you. Imagine talking to that person. In the conversation, be sure to tell the person about your *real* feelings. Tell the person how his or her behavior has made you feel in the past. DO NOT apologize, minimize, or feel guilty for expressing your emotions, especially the negative ones. Pause for a moment. Are all of your feelings about the person out on the table now? Do you need to say more? Are you sure? Now, imagine telling the person that you are going to try your best to forgive him or her and to release your negative feelings. Imagine telling that person, but only because you truly feel it, that you forgive him or her and can release your negative emotions.

When you have completed the visualization process for a particular person, write "FORGIVEN" across the small piece of paper and tear it up, or, better yet, burn it. Here again, it is crucial not to jump over your feelings in order to get to the resolution phase of forgiveness. The tendency to rush toward forgiveness at your own expense is within you; go slowly!

As you watch the smoke, or hold the torn pieces of paper, imagine that all of your bad feelings and blocked energy have been set free through forgiveness. Forgiving another allows us to forgive ourselves.

Write a letter to your alcoholic parent(s) in which you list all of the things that you always used to wish (and probably still do) that they had done or been for you. This letter is *not* meant to be given to your parent(s).

Next, spend some time looking at and feeling the sadness and disappointment surrounding each of the things you wished for. Repeat an affirmation to yourself on each point, "I mourn and release my sadness and longing," until you can visualize yourself forgiving your parent(s) and feeling released from your grief. Burn the letter when you have finished the exercise.

This exercise will not miraculously relieve all of your feelings of neediness and wanting, but it will help you to direct your healing powers to the place where mourning needs to take place.

Make a list of small pleasures that bring joy into your life. Here are some of mine.

Letters from friends.

Puppies' faces.

Being picked up at the airport when I come home.

Warm baths with plenty of time for wallowing.

Waking up to the sound of birds.

Taking a nap.

Music—harp and flute.

The smell of wood smoke on my clothes.

Write down as many things as you can think of. Then take a look at your list. How many of these little pleasures currently exist in your life? Which ones could you reasonably add to your daily life? Are there any unhealthy or potentially unhealthy items/activities on your list? How many of the things that you enjoy involve another person? Is this inclusion/exclusion of another person intentional on your part?

Does This Playpen Come In Extra Large?

* * *

Describe a problem or a situation in your life that you want to work on, to improve.

List any emotions you feel as you do this. Not just your thoughts.

List any physical sensation that you feel while writing the list (cold feet, tight chest, prickly skin).

List your thoughts. What internal messages are you beginning to hear?

Write down the worst thing that could happen. What do you fear the most? Then try imagining that the worst thing happened. Next, imagine the next worst thing and imagine that it did happen. Go on and on with this imagining.

Write down what is the best thing that could happen. Describe your ideal scene. See it clearly, feel it, taste it, touch it.

What fear or negative belief is keeping you from creating what you want? Hint: Look back on the worst-thing scenarios.

Write down your negative belief as precisely as you can state it. Write down as many negative beliefs as you can find.

Then create a countermessage, the positive flipside of each negative belief. Make these messages short and in the present tense. Use your name in them, like for affirmations. After all, you are talking to yourself, and you want to make sure that you have your attention.

Say your positive messages silently to yourself while visualizing the problems in your life turning out the way you want. Expect success!

If you find negative thoughts creeping in while you do this exercise, and you probably will, try to counteract them with reverse, positive messages.

Remember the permission slips you had to get as a child? Permission to be late to school, be excused early, to be dismissed from class. Now, try writing your own permission slips. You may want to paste these permission slips around the house where you can see them, or carry them with you for quick reference.

I, _____, give myself permission to feel and to show my feelings.

I, _____, give myself permission to change my mind. I do not have to stick to bad decisions.

I, _____, give myself permission to not feel responsible for other people.

I, _____, give myself permission to say "no" when I want to.

I, _____, give myself permission to stand up for my rights.

I, _____, give myself permission to not be perfect all the time.

I, _____, give myself permission to disappoint other people some times if my needs must come first.

Make up your own permission slips based on the particular areas where you are not very permissive with yourself.

Creative visualization and affirmations are tools aimed toward the goal of improvement and change. An aim is a specific mental attitude that asks, "What do I want?" A goal is the answer to that question. A goal demands specificity and the formulation of a plan to ensure its attainment. A general goal such as, "I want to feel better," is too broad and too vague. A plan of action will be difficult to develop for such a goal. However, a more specific goal, such as "I want to stop reacting in such an automatic manner whenever my mother calls me on the phone," is a clear and workable goal. A very important point to remember, which may be new information for ACOAs, is that goals and desires DO NOT REQUIRE JUSTIFICATION OR EXPLANATION. I have a friend whose mother used to insist that she write essays to explain and justify her actions and desires when she was a teenager. This woman still has trouble setting reasonable goals for herself. She imagines that any stated desire is an inflexible demand upon her. She feels the need to succeed at everything or else be held up to harsh criticism. Her accumulated anxiety over setting goals keeps her from trying new things and taking risks in her life. It also keeps her from experiencing much of what she truly longs for in life.

A great deal of the goal-setting that went on during our childhoods was aimed at securing survival and a sense of safety in our alcoholic homes. But in adulthood these goals become inflexible and self-destructive. The goals we forged in childhood need to be readjusted toward the purposes of healthy adult life. The realization of the personal cost of adapting within an alcoholic family allows us to establish ideas of where we would rather be, how we would rather feel, and what we really want to be doing with our lives. Self-observation, journal work, and listening to our inner voices will all provide information about the adaptations we made as children.

Goal setting is very much like the process of creative visualization. Begin by stating a goal for yourself. State it as though it already were a fact, in the present tense. Next, write down some reasons why you cannot have what you want. List anything that comes into your head. Do not edit anything, regardless of how much you wish it hadn't shown up.

> GOAL: I am an artist, making a living by doing what I love the best.
>
>> INTERFERENCE: I can't draw.
>>
>> No one makes a decent living as an artist.
>>
>> No one will buy my work.
>>
>> Artists are not respected members of society.

After generating your counterproductive messages, spend some time looking at the list. Which messages seem most powerful to you? Hint: Have you heard any of these messages verbalized by either of your parents? Pick

the most powerful negative message and write a counteracting affirmative statement.

> "My intuition influences my art, it touches people
> and they respond positively. I am a success."

   Once a desired outcome can be visualized, and the
internal rebellion quelled through the use of affirmations,
a plan of action for achieving your desired outcome must
be established. Without this plan of action, any goal is
just wishful thinking. Your plan of action should be
clear, while remaining flexible enough to allow for
changes and adjustments that may need to be made.
However, flexibility is not a noted characteristic of
ACOAs, so it is important to keep watching for your
own resistance and sabotage.
   Personally, I think that the plan of action is where fear
and doubt hide. It is where the "What if . . . ?" messages lurk. To get a clear example, take a piece of paper
and list five to ten things you would like to do or accomplish in the next two years. On the back of the paper
write down anything that is presently keeping you from
having or achieving those desires. Whenever we begin to
look at our dreams and wishes, we begin to hear internal
complaints. "Oh, I could never do that . . . It costs too
much money . . . I don't know enough . . . What would
other people think? . . . I'm not good enough." This is
because we have a vast repository of disappointed wishes
and dreams. The tendency to say, "Yes, but . . ." is a
protective buffer against disappointment and anticipoint-

ment. Start listening to the complaints, but don't give them too much power. Try imagining, as Freeme can, that there are no barriers in reality, only in your head. Picture being able to step right over or through the barriers. Imagine and expect your success. Formulate an affirmation and repeat it to yourself whenever the image of your success begins to fade. Begin to trust yourself and your potential. Adult children must relearn their power. They are no longer children, forced to internalize the message, "Nothing I do will make the drinking stop," or "Nothing I do will make them stop fighting." The messages now need to say, "I was never responsible for the drinking, and I will not allow the choices of my parents to negatively affect my life. I am free to make my own choices without feeling as though I am betraying my family." Practice with creative visualization will boost self-confidence, eliminate doubt and worry, and produce positive results. Picture yourself in your mind's eye just as you wish to be, doing exactly what you dream of, and eventually you will come to see yourself doing and being just that.

An exercise that I have found helpful when I am feeling lost and out of focus is to spend fifteen to twenty minutes writing about what would be an ideal day for me. I write continuously, without giving myself a chance to justify or edit what comes out. I write in the first person and describe the place that I am in, who else is there, and how I spend my time, no matter how fanciful or improbable it seems. Looking back over what I have written invariably illuminates desires and goals that I have hidden behind my day-to-day reality. It is these hidden desires and goals that we need to rediscover and honor. They are part of us, and even if we cannot have everything we want right this minute, we deserve to dream, to want and to expect that we will receive.

Each and every one of us *deserves* to have dreams and desires. We are no longer children, and we are not victims, doomed to respond and react to another's behavior like robots. We have choices and power and unlimited resources for creating the present and the future of our dreams. It is possible to convert the energy that once went into worry and fear into the energy that can heal and make whole.

Recovery is not a goal, but rather a process, a journey. There is a beginning but no clear end. The process of recovery involves changing what once felt oppressive into an opportunity for investigation and change. By taking responsibility, it is possible to refashion the present and leave behind the influence of the past. It is possible to risk vulnerability and thereby open oneself to the possibility of intimacy. And it is possible to play, create, and have fun without feeling guilty or scared.

Awareness and the process of recovery started for me during the guided imagery session that I described at the beginning of this book. At that time I did not accept the responsibility and chose, out of fear, to turn away from my past and keep trying to forge ahead without looking back. However, my desire for more intimacy, fun, and creative expression in my life made it impossible to continue to ignore the fact that I needed to go back into my childhood home, look around with adult eyes, shed the denial, and mourn for what had not been available.

169

Today I can accept both the sad and the joyous parts of the process. It is my sincere hope that something in this book has sparked your interest and your desire to take that first step, rather than continue turning away from the challenge. Plenty of help and support is available if you can bring yourself to ask for it. Getting started and accepting responsibility for changing your life is hard, but the journey toward recovery is well worth every single step.

Bibliography

Ackerman, Robert J. *Children of Alcoholics,* Holmes Beach, Florida: Learning Publications, Inc., 1983

Baldwin, Christina. *One to One: Self-Understanding Through Journal Work,* New York: M. Evans & Co., 1977

Berkeley Holistic Health Center. *The Holistic Health Handbook,* Berkeley: AND/OR Press, 1978

Bettelheim, Bruno. *The Uses of Enchantment,* New York: Vintage Books, 1977

Black, Claudia. *It Will Never Happen To Me!,* Denver: M.A.C. Printing & Publications, 1981

Black, Claudia. *Repeat After Me,* Denver: M.A.C. Printing & Publications, 1985

Butler, Pamela E. *Talking To Yourself,* San Francisco: Harper & Row Publishers, 1981

Capacchione, Lucia. *The Creative Journal,* Athens, Ohio: Swallow Press, 1979

Deutsch, Charles. *Broken Bottles, Broken Dreams,* New York: Teachers College Press, 1982

Downey, Bill. *Right Brain-Write On,* Englewood Cliffs, NJ: Prentice-Hall, Inc., 1984

Edwards, David D. *How To Be More Creative,* Los Gatos, CA: Occasional Productions, 1979

Elkind, David. *The Hurried Child,* Reading, PA: Addison-Wesley Publishing Co., 1981

Fraiberg, Selma H. *The Magic Years,* New York: Charles Scribner's Sons, 1959

Gawain, Shakti. *The Creative Visualization Workbook,* Mill Valley: Whatever Publishing, Inc., 1982

171

Houston, Jean. *The Possible Human*, Los Angeles: J. P. Tarcher, Inc., 1982

Lerner, Rokelle. *Daily Affirmations for Adult Children of Alcoholics*, Pompano Beach, FL: Health Communications, Inc., 1985

Lowen, Alexander. *Narcissism: Denial of the True Self*, New York: Collier Books, 1983

May, Rollo. *The Courage To Create*, Toronto: Bantam Books, 1975

Miller, Alice. *The Drama of The Gifted Child*, New York: Basic Books Inc., 1981

Minuchin, Salvador. *Family Kaleidoscope*, Cambridge: Harvard University Press, 1984

Missildine, W. Hugh, MD. *Your Inner Child of the Past*, New York: Pocket Books, 1963

Norwood, Robin. *Women Who Love Too Much*, New York: Pocket Books, 1985

O'Connor, Elizabeth. *Our Many Selves*, New York: Harper & Row, 1971

Peck, M. Scott. *The Road Less Traveled*, New York: Simon & Schuster, 1978

Reid, Clyde H. *Dreams*, Minneapolis: Winston Press, Inc., 1983

Robbins, Lois B. *Waking Up In The Age of Creativity*, Santa Fe: Bear & Company, 1985

Ryan, Regina Sara, & Travis, John W., MD. *Wellness Workbook*, Berkeley: Ten Speed Press, 1981

Samples, Bob. *The Metaphoric Mind*, Reading, PA: Addison-Wesley Publishing Co., 1976

Seixas, Judith S. & Youcha, Geraldine. *Children of Alcoholism: A Survivor's Manual*, New York: Crown Publishers, Inc., 1985

Shapiro, Stephen, & Ryglewicz, Hilary. *Feeling Safe*, Englewood Cliffs, NJ: Prentice-Hall, Inc., 1976

Sher, Barbara. *Wishcraft*, New York: Ballantine Books, 1979

Shone, Ronald. *Creative Visualization*, New York: Thorsons Publishers, Inc., 1984

Simonton, O. Carl, MD., Matthews-Simonton, Stephanie, & Creighton, James L. *Getting Well Again*, Toronto: Bantam Books, 1978

Bibliography

Wegscheider-Cruse, Sharon. *Choice-Making,* Pompano Beach, FL: Health Communications, Inc., 1985

Wheelis, Allen. *How People Change,* New York: Harper Colophon Books, 1973

Woititz, Janet Geringer. *Adult Children of Alcoholics,* Hollywood, FL: Health Communications, Inc., 1983

Woititz, Janet Geringer. *Struggle For .... Intimacy,* Pompano Beach, FL: Health Communications, Inc., 1985

About the Author

Had Megan LeBoutillier conducted the research for LITTLE MISS PERFECT in a formal setting, she would have earned "several advanced degrees." Motivated by a desire to understand why her creativity was blocked, she found the answer in the dysfunction of her childhood home. Her commitment to deepening her own recovery resulted in the writing of this book.

Ms. LeBoutillier lives on Pawleys Island, South Carolina, with her husband, where she is presently writing a book about the puzzle of personal boundaries in recovery.

SOBERING INSIGHT FOR THE ALCOHOLIC . . . AND THE LOVED ONES WHO WANT TO HELP THEM